Music Row Dogs & Nashville Cats

Country Stars and Their Pets

KAREN WILL ROGERS

LAURA LACY

CMT

Pocket Books

New York   London   Toronto   Sydney

CMT

POCKET BOOKS, a division of Simon & Schuster, Inc.
1230 Avenue of the Americas, New York, NY 10020
CMT © 2004 Country Music Television, Inc., a division
of MTV Networks, a Viacom company.

ISBN: 0-7434-9193-9

First CMT/Pocket Books trade paperback edition June 2004

10   9   8   7   6   5   4   3   2   1

POCKET and colophon are registered trademarks of
Simon & Schuster, Inc.

Manufactured in the United States of America

For information regarding special discounts for bulk purchases, please contact
Simon & Schuster Special Sales at 1-800-456-6798 or business@simonandschuster.com

All photographs courtesy of Karen Will Rogers,
except for page 148, taken by Herb Burnett, and pages 160 and 161,
taken by Nancy Lee Andrews.

Contents

Foreword

What would our world be like without animals, especially those that have become close friends—our pets? Many of us can't imagine our lives without a furry friend climbing onto our lap—indeed, pets enhance our outlook on life itself! How many times have you come home exhausted from a hard day at work to find your best animal friend at the door to greet you with tail wagging? Now, that's a definite mood elevator!

Pets are really important for children: caring for a cat, dog, or guinea pig teaches the lessons of responsibility, patience, loyalty, and love.

As busy as my wife, Suzi, and I have been over the years, rearing three daughters, acting as Director of the Columbus Zoo, and traveling the world filming *Animal Adventures*, we've always had pets in our lives. We couldn't imagine it any other way. Pets are woven into the fabric of our existence—they are playful, delightful, and loving. Enjoy *Music Row Dogs & Nashville Cats*—you'll get an up-close and personal look at many of your favorite country stars with their favorite critters!

JACK HANNA
Director Emeritus, Columbus Zoo
Host, *Jack Hanna's Animal Adventures*

Introduction

In 1998, Nashville, Tennessee, a major city producing legendary music artists for more than five decades, rich in history and American culture, had a 30-year-old animal shelter that was mismanaged, in horrific condition, and sorely neglected. The fact that it was a government-run facility made it even worse. Karen Will Rogers, an animal lover and photographer, convinced the interim director to allow her to photographically document the abominable conditions. When the photos hit the front-page news and air waves, it stunned the city. Our findings generated an amazing response from some highly recognizable faces, including country music stars, media, city council members, and animal rights activists. This group aggressively yet peacefully protested, and convinced the then-mayor, Phil Bredesen, to find funding for a new shelter facility. With the passionate help of country stars Lorrie Morgan, Barbara Mandrell, Gary Chapman, and Natalie Maines, naming just a few, we now have a new state-of-the-art facility, run by a caring, committed staff. The kill rate has dropped dramatically since the new shelter was constructed, from 98% at the old shelter to 35% and falling. We hope it will soon be 0%.

This book pays homage to all who care enough to spay, neuter, rescue, and adopt animals, and to the country music industry, for standing behind the cause and making a difference in their community. Thank you to some of the most deeply spiritual people we will ever know.

We encourage anyone who is considering acquiring a new pet to please support your local humane association or shelter. It will change your life and save a life. We hope this book will inspire you to engage in community efforts, no matter what the cause. Do anything, you pick it! For us, it was our love for people, music, and the love of animals.

KAREN WILL ROGERS
LAURA LACY

Rhett Akins

"I've had tons of dogs, and to me they were always truly man's best friend. Every dog I had would follow me to the ends of the earth. Even if they ran off, they would always come back—they're completely loyal. I had outdoor dogs that ran alongside my four wheeler, runnin' at thirty-five miles an hour—their lungs ready to burst, had to have been. They'd go swimming, splashing in the river, jumpin' in the pond, then hang out in the back of the truck. They'd walk with me in the woods and sit out with me on the porch. I love dogs to be free and enjoy everything about the outdoors.

"When I think about humans and animals, I always go back to the Bible. God gave Adam dominion over the animals in the field, and I don't think it was God's intention for us to treat animals cruelly. I think we're here to protect and honor."

The Bellamy Brothers

Howard Bellamy

"Socks just wandered up to the barn and never left. We have lots of animals that do that. My mom has fifteen or twenty cats. People just come out to the country and drop off strays, and we take care of the ones we can and spay or neuter them.

"Candy is our Jack Russell. She's named after our friend who found her. We had two Jack Russells for about fifteen years, and we loved them a lot. They are so smart. Candy hangs out with me in my office, and she's a great protector and watchdog. We just got hooked on Jack Russells; they have a certain personality that goes well with the rest of the family. It's always fun.

"We do the absolute best we can to take good care of these animals.

There is nothing worse than to see animals in bad condition. It's like seeing a starving child; it is awful. They are family. We think as much of a dog in our family as we do each other. Yes, we've had quite the cast of characters between the cats, the dogs, the cattle, and the horses. The stories are endless. We've done the best we can and will continue to do so. That will never change."

Dierks Bentley

"I found Jake at the Nashville Pound. He was two days away from being put down, and even though I wasn't looking for a dog at the time, when I saw him we just clicked. So I figured, 'Well, okay.' He's been a big part of my life ever since.

"He was there when I went through a breakup and I credit him for helping me get through that time. I'd come home after being in the studio and we'd go to the park and hang out, just the two of us. He was there when I wrote a lot of songs that are on my album. He was a huge part of my healing, and helped me work through a lot of stuff. He brought me joy when things didn't seem very joyful.

"Jake likes to learn and is quick to pick up on things. We have so much fun on the bus; he's provided hours of endless entertainment. That's his way of giving back. When I go to writing appointments, he comes, too. I guess I need to give him a writing credit, because he's always there in the room. He comes to sound check with me at shows, too. Plus he gets recognized, so he's helping my career. I think he's helped me sell a few more albums.

"I wish everyone would look at their dog as if they're children. Don't do anything to your pet that you wouldn't do to your child. They need to be respected, just like people. I feel like God brought Jake into my life when I was going through a lot of difficult times. He's been there when things were really bad, and he's still here and a part of all the fun we're having now. I'm just so thankful that he came into my life when he did. He's happy, thankful, and loving—and I guess that rubs off on you!"

Clint Black and Lisa Hartman Black

"I remember a rainy Sunday morning when we lived in LA, and our housekeeper called and said that she had found a little puppy in the street, in the gutter. I told her to bring him home and we would find a home for him. Clint was in the shower and when I took the puppy upstairs and held him up to Clint, he looked out of the shower and said, 'Oh, we have to keep him.' His name is Radar, and he's a big guy and a wonderful dog. All of my life I have brought dogs home, and thank goodness I have such a great mom, who let me keep them all.

"When we were in Nashville one time, Clint was on the road, so I went to a shelter just to walk some of the animals. Well, I fell in love and brought one home with me. Clint and I feel that love is defined by caring for those who can't care for themselves. There are no boundaries to pets' love. But they can't tell us what they feel, so we need to pay close attention to them.

"We are very affectionate with our dogs and spend a lot of time with them, lots of hands-on love and attention. We go to the park, and our daughter, Lilly, plays with them all the time. She will lie down and put her head next to theirs; oh, they love her. She has learned the value of being kind and gentle with our pets, who are like playmates for her. Aside from your family, there is nothing more rewarding than animals and music."

Paul Brandt

"Baileigh is a chow-shar-pei mix. We went to visit friends who had just gotten her and it was pouring rain. In the backyard, she was playing on a garbage can lid filled with water from the rain. She was all in it, having a great time, and she was the cutest thing I'd ever seen. I just fell in love with Baileigh. We started playing with her and our friends said, 'Ya know, we thought this was a good idea but we can't take care of her.' I said no, but of course my wife, Liz, said yes.

"Baileigh's taught me so much about not focusing on myself, and for a music artist, that is a really big deal! Animals can be destructive and she has ruined some of my things, but I think that also teaches you that things aren't that important.

"Baileigh's been on the road since she was four months old and she's ten now. She's been the best road dog in the whole wide world. Sometimes my family can't come on tour with me, but to know Baileigh's waiting there on the bus when I come off the stage, ready to hit the next town, is just awesome. It's great to have that friendship."

13

T. Graham Brown

"We had a rat terrier growing up. After I moved away from home, I didn't have a pet until Sheila, my wife, found Snoopy. My son, Acme, picked him out and named him. I always wanted a dog that would fetch, and this dog can fetch! He chases

squirrels and starts to holler like beagles do, but he's a big ol' housedog. He sleeps with us at night. We just love him; he's a big part of our life. You better take care of animals, because you never know, you may come back as one. So treat them like somebody.

"We have pet friends, a little sheltie that lives down the street and a pug, and they come over and hang out with Snoopy. They're just like our son and his friends; it's a riot. You'll see them hanging out in the neighborhood together and sometimes they run and play. If you watch them together, it's like a cartoon. What a good laugh! Entertainment in a pure, natural form."

BR549

Geoff Firebaugh

"They are just awesome. I adore them. If Lily could talk, she would say, 'Give me treats; ignore that other dog, I am the queen.' She's a rescue who was headed to death row. We took other dogs from someone who was abusing them. I was so angry, I wanted a piece of the guy.

"I'm truly dedicated to these loving creatures; they are a part of me. I feel the pain and see the tragedy and fright in the eyes of a homeless animal.

"Extend yourself. Go get an animal that needs a home!"

Chuck Mead

"I can't imagine life without some sort of pet running around. Jack is demanding and he wishes he were the only cat. I love them both. We've domesticated animals, so it is our responsibility to look after and take care of them. That's where spaying and neutering comes in. Love, attention, and nurturing—isn't that what it's all about?"

Shaw Wilson

"I'm the godfather of these dogs, and I love them. It is bitter that I'm allergic to them, but it doesn't deplete my love for them.

"They do the craziest things. They have their own personalities, and they don't get enough credit for that. People who mistreat animals cheat themselves; they are missing out on surprises and a lot of insights about being a creature on earth. 'Cause that's what we all are."

Tracy Byrd

"I rescued Lucy by way of my long-time manager, Joe Carter. I've got two Labs, named Maggie and Sadie, a little Yorkie, a cat, and we just lost a dog, too. Still, we've got a houseful and that's the way we like it. A house full of love. They just light up when they see us, they get so excited. You can see it all over their faces. They smile. Oh, they've been so good for my kids. They've taught my kids about respect.

"All I have to do is come outside in my camouflage, and my hunting dogs, Maggie and Sadie, go crazy. They are so smart, they know we're going hunting. They understand exactly what their role is and they love it. It makes them happy.

"My wife, Michelle, is incredible. She's got the biggest heart; she picks up strays and finds them homes. By looking into an animal's eyes you can tell what it's feeling, just like us. They get their feelings hurt, just like we do. And the least little thing you do can make them happy. Please spread the word to take better care in loving animals. I care, I take responsibility, and so does my family."

Deana Carter

"**I** worked double shifts to help pay for my miniature pinscher, Gibson. I found him in a pet store and instantly fell in love with him. I wanted him so badly; I literally went into hock to get him.

"Gibby brings me so much joy and laughter; he is definitely my baby. When he was a puppy, I'd put him in my shirt to keep him warm. I've tried to break him of the habit, but I give in, what can I say? He's stubborn and pig-headed sometimes, just like his momma, and the least little bit he overeats, it shows. He's so smart, he's learned how to knock on the door with one paw while Bette, my German shepherd, rings the bells on the door. Bette's more shy than Gibby, more sensitive.

"I love all animals. I just don't understand why we humans tend to think we are the big deal here on earth. The whole issue of mankind forgetting the essence of why we're here really bugs me. We're not the end-all and be-all on this planet. So, please, reach out and adopt or rescue. Pets are truly the most wonderful companions."

Gary Chapman

"I'm a big supporter of Happy Trails. It is a no-kill, privately funded organization here in Nashville. My wife, Jennifer, and I spend a lot of time helping out with events and day-to-day tasks.

"Our big guy, Simon, is very vocal, but a gentle giant. He has become very protective of his space, but he is still very gentle. He loves piling in with us and the kids. It's pretty funny. When we wake up in the morning, he talks to us, like, how you doing? I mean, he is *vocal!* We adopted him.

We were told they were very loving animals and they are.

"I genuinely care about animals. It's a way of life I want to practice, and I want my kids to learn it on this level—so that when they are faced with a human crisis, their natural reaction will be to do something about it. I want them to learn compassion by taking care of our animals. It's the lessons we carry over to them that will allow them to benefit."

Charlie Chase

"**O**ur pets rule our home. My wife, Karen, and I are just happy that they are gracious enough to let us live here. Rodney, Lacy, and Sherlock have complete run of the house—three stories, several staircases, and an elevator. They all have their own room but prefer to sleep in the same room as Karen and me.

"Rodney, our black and white sheltie, was named after our favorite comedian, Rodney Dangerfield. We found Lacy, the Maltese, at a pet store. I think she was trained to sucker us into adopting her, with her unforgettable eyes and adoring nature. Sherlock, our chow and sheepdog mix, was found standing in the middle of a busy road in Brentwood. We didn't want him to get injured, so Karen opened the car door and he jumped in. Once we got home, he ran away as soon as that car door opened. But lo and behold, a week later he came back covered in mud, briars, and wire. He lay completely still while Karen patiently groomed him for nine hours straight. We tried for weeks to find his owners but no one ever claimed him. He greets us every day when we come home. He became family instantly; we consider all our pets family.

"We cannot understand neglect and abuse. Dogs are full of love; they are always happy to see you and there is a comfort in knowing they're there. Dogs are not just living creatures, they are caring creatures, and can truly be your best friend. If more people thought of them that way, it would make a huge difference."

Mark Chesnutt

"Here I am with my buddy, Champion. He's a friend's dog, but he represents all my dogs back home in Texas. I'm on the road and I wanted to stand behind this book. The love and care for a pet is a cause that each and every one of us should pay attention to. I've got quite a few dogs but my pal, Calvin, my chow, has been with me for fourteen years. He's still doing great; heck, he's outlived all my other ten dogs. I'm waiting for my chow puppy; she's a Christmas present from my wife, Tracie. Her name's Tinker. And we just got a longhaired dachshund

named Jessi. She was Waylon Jennings's dog, and he named her after his wife, Jessie Colter Jennings.

"I've rescued aplenty—it's a wonder my wife lets me come home anymore! One time I was home for a few days and I was going in and out of town for different things. Every day I'd go past this one railroad crossing, and every day I would see this dog sittin' in the same place. He'd look at me and I'd look at him and I'd go on about my business. Well, after about three days of that, I finally looked at him and said, 'Get in'; so he jumped in the back of the truck and we never looked back. Animals make it all good. Next time you see a big ol' sweet face that needs a home, you pick him up. You may need him more than he needs you!"

Terri Clark

"Oscar goes everywhere with me; he's my little Mr. Man. Heck, I was tired of sleeping alone so I went to the shelter and rescued him. He looks like a cross between a basset hound and a dachshund, hence the name Oscar, for a weiner dog. He stood out from the other dogs when he sat up on his hind legs and did a balancing act on his tail, and the rest is history.

"I take him on the road, and everywhere we go, everyone falls in love with him. The first time my friend, Beth Neilsen Chapman, saw Oscar she said, 'What a cute poopy,' and the nickname Poopy Pants was born. He sleeps with me and loves to burrow under the covers. He keeps me warm at night and has probably kept me out of a lot of dysfunctional relationships. He hates being alone and jumps into the car whenever he gets the chance. Once he's in the car, it's a bit of a challenge getting him out until we go somewhere. I think he must have separation anxiety.

"I cannot imagine life without him. It would have been such a loss if I hadn't saved him from the shelter, where his time was almost up. I really wish more people would put thought into the responsibility of owning a pet; you can't decide to get a pet and expect it to take care of itself. I want to save them all, and I'm just thankful I could save one."

Katie Cook

CMT Host

"Sateen is a rescue, fully blind, and old, old. Geddy Lee is a rescue from the Humane Society and we named her after the lead singer of Rush because he has that long, skinny nose. Our little chow—our east Nashville mix, as we like to call him—is Huggy Bear. He was rescued by our friend Joshua Ragsdale, and we fell in love with him.

"If I've had a bad day and my husband, Mark, is on the road, I still know that I'm going to see smiling faces and wagging tails when I walk in the door. It's almost like having kids, the way it teaches you to be selfless. I take care of them no matter what. Even if I'm tired or sick, it doesn't matter, they need my love—and they give back the 'I'd do anything for you' kinda love that I couldn't live without. They entertain us, too. We hardly even turn the television on when we first get home, because they're so happy to see us, they show off and perform for us. Just give them a tennis ball and the show begins.

"Their image of me is so simple and innocent: I'm kinda their world, and that's a heavy responsibility. Pets trust us so, and we owe it to them to give them the most incredible life. If we are truly an evolving race, with all of our technology and our advances, we cannot possibly leave animals behind; we must be compassionate and look out for them. If everyone who wanted a pet would just go to the pound instead of the mall, and everyone would spay and neuter, we could all make a difference. Just think twice. And spread the word. Educate your kids; take them to the shelter, show them how those animals live, teach them compassion for living creatures at an early age. It will teach them love and appreciation in other ways, too."

Billy Ray Cyrus

"These dogs are three of my best friends. Two came from the shelter, Sheba and Fluke, and both have been great dogs. I've had Sheba for ten years and she has absolutely been the most loyal friend a person could ask for. I think Sheba knows she was rescued; she has been very grateful and there is no doubt that she would give her life for me.

"Anywhere I go around here, these dogs go with me, every inch of the way. When I drive that mule, they stay right with me. Lucky doesn't really come out and run the hills; she's kinda fufu. But these guys, they're the pack, they are part of the land.

"I lost a dog in 2001, my big collie, Pawnee. I had her for years. When I was in Toronto working on my show *Doc*, I was stranded because of the events of 9/11. Pawnee had a serious phobia of loud noises like gunshots and thunder, and I wasn't here to put her up when hunting season came in that fall, and we also had severe weather then. She had a heart attack and died. This is the first photo session I've done without Pawnee, so I'm feeling a little sad today. I think the other dogs miss her, too, I think they wonder where she is, ya know? I have no doubt that if I'd been home to put her up, she would be here today. 9/11 affected us all, even our animals. So in a way, my family was a casualty, too.

"My very first band in 1980 was called Sly Dog. I had an old mutt with one eye, exactly

like Spirit here. Well, one night after band rehearsal, me and my band were at my mom's house in Flatt Woods, Kentucky, and we were all contemplating what we were gonna call the band. My mutt rolled over and the drummer, his name was Bubba, looked down and said, 'You old sly dog, you.' I said, 'That's it, that's it. That's the name of this band.' And to this day, that is the name of my band. You talk about things going full circle, here's ol' Sly Dog laying right there in the mule, with one eye—so 20 years later, I still have a one-eyed dog and a band called Sly Dog. I kept telling Spirit to stay away from this little donkey we have, but Spirit kept standing behind him, barking. I told him that one day that donkey was gonna knock his eye out, and sure as hell, one day he did.

"I don't have three more loyal companions than these dogs. If you love your pets, they will love you back."

In loving memory of my dear friend Pawnee.

34

The Dancehall Doctors

Jeff McMahon

"Pets can be so quick to forgive, whether you're justified in scolding them, or whether you're just taking something out on them and say things you don't mean. If you treat them well, generally when you reach that door, they are right there. If they're not, that means that something is wrong—they must be sick or trapped under

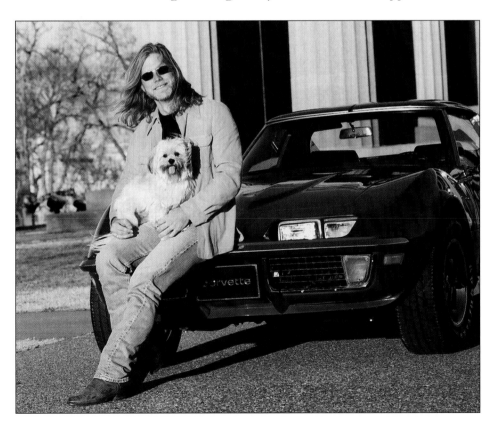

something heavy. That's how much they forgive and how much they love.

"I've seen people who would place their pet before another person. At the same time, I've seen people who don't have time for their own cat or dog, yet they want to have children. Hello! They don't even walk their *dog*— what are they thinkin'? A pet has to be a priority; there is a soul there.

"I had a golden retriever when I was growing up named Muffin. If she was afraid of thunder or anything, she'd always come upstairs and find me. The upstairs was off-limits to the dog, but I kinda catered to her. As an adult, I realize my dad knew she was upstairs, even though we thought we were getting away with something.

"Boomer, our current family dog, was a rescue. The lady who owned him just decided that she didn't want to go through the hassle of house-breaking him, so she dropped him off at the shelter the day my parents went looking for a dog. The shelter goes to such lengths for their screening process . . . they faxed forms back and forth, and even did background checks before my folks finally got the dog.

"I love this dog. I don't see him as much as I want to, but I do spend a lot of time in Texas with my family. I guess I need to get a wife before I get a dog of my own; I'm just gone so much. That's the whole point of having a pet—sharing experiences with them, seeing them respond to you, and allowing yourself to respond to them. There are plenty of people who do what I do that have pets, but there's still a family for the pet to belong to when they're gone. With Boomer, he's with family all the time, and that's the way it should be. I still have him in my life, and that's a gift. That's why I had to go to Texas and bring him to Nashville for this book. I guess you could say I went the extra mile, or in this case, the extra *six hundred* miles for him.

"So I get to share this with my family. Even Li'l Bit, my niece who isn't reading yet, carries around pictures of our family . . . and she'd be looking for him. The point of this book is not only the rescue element, but also how animals impact people. And Boomer doesn't just impact our family . . . he is part of it."

Charlie Daniels

"I've had so many dogs through the years. I love ol' dogs. There is something so special about a dog. I think a dog, more than any other animal, can be a friend and demonstrate the way that he feels about you.

"They have taught me something about love; I'm sure of that. I love it when they come up and rub on you, let you know they're there, kinda smilin' up at ya. They love going places with you, walking with you, and just enjoy being with you—that's love. Why, we'll take Beezle with us in the car, where we've got a child seat for our godson, and Beezle seems to like it an awful lot, too: he'll get in that thing and ride in it. I guess he likes the view from there. We used to have a poodle that would ring the bell when he wanted to go outside. They are so smart.

"They are our good friends, they are good friends to our children. A dog is just the best pet you could ever have."

Linda Davis

"There are so many people who get great joy from pets. I've noticed so many older people with dogs lately; their pets must be a constant source of companionship for them. Little ones love pets, too. To watch my daughter play with them is so precious. She'll be saying 'puppy, puppy' for a week.

"I so want to see this beautiful shelter puppy find a home. Right now I'm on the road so much, it wouldn't be right. If you're not going to take care of them, don't take on the responsibility. God put them here to be our little sidekicks, to be our friends. We need to love and enjoy them."

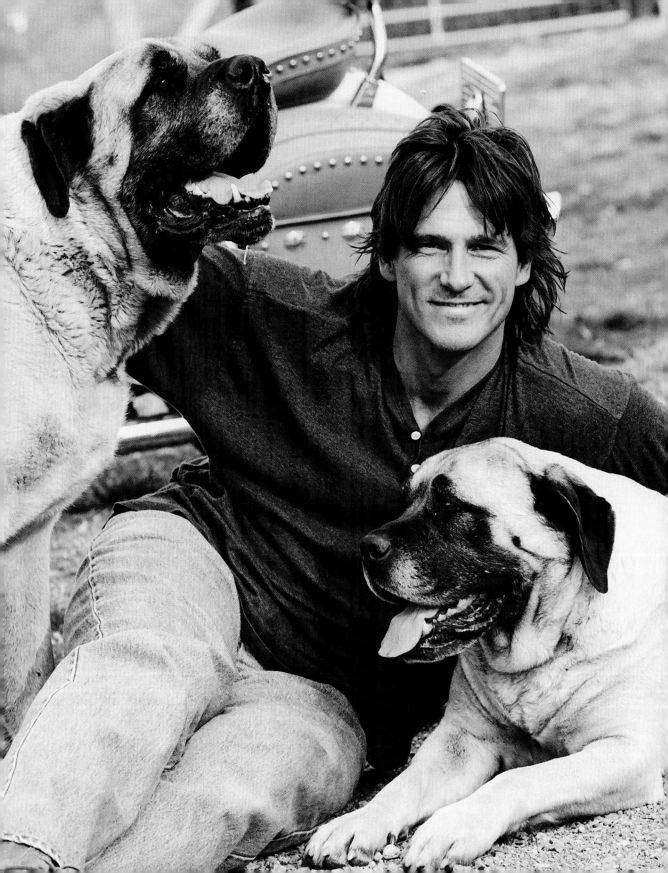

Billy Dean

"At a McDonald's in Colorado, there was a truck in front of us that had cages. Inside was what looked like little bears. The people were breeders, and I told them I wanted to buy two of the mastiff puppies. I had small children at the time and the puppies were so gentle with the kids, not aggressive at all. They grew up on my farm. I wanted to give them an extraordinary life—a big place to run and a big lake to cool off in during summer. Their life span is about eight years, Bonnie and Clyde are eleven, but we lost Bonnie this year. She had a great life, though. They've had run-ins with everything: opossum, raccoons, skunks, you name it, and they've run into it. They chased and hunted and they had a ball.

"I give them body massages, and when I gave Bonnie her last massage it was one of those weird spiritual moments. I could tell she wasn't gonna be around much longer. It was like, 'Daddy, I'm ready to go.' I'm glad she went the way she did; she died in her sleep. We buried her in the primo spot on the farm. The best view, the highest point, under a beautiful tree. We celebrated her life. The dogs have both been my family, along with my kids. We are a unit.

"I learned so much about old age from them, that you have to let nature take its course. We would always walk the mile and a half to the lake and I loved that time with them. It was good for us, and our souls.

"We're very lucky and privileged to share the planet with these amazing animals. It teaches us that we are not here alone. When my kids were having trouble with my divorce, they would go outside and talk to the dogs, just sit with them, and the dogs would listen to them. Dogs are good therapy and good friends.

"Just remember that the good Lord put us in charge and to be responsible to watch over them. It is a good way to teach us about selflessness. So spay and neuter your pets, and guys, don't take it personal—it's not you being neutered!"

Diamond Rio

Jimmy Olander

"Elvis lived a great and long life. Claudia and I got him at six days because he was sick and we bottle-fed him and nursed him. We cried ourselves to sleep many a night, 'cause it was really tough going. He barely made it, but he did: to 176 whopping pounds and eleven years old. He was king of the roost. Heck, we got rid of the dining room furniture and replaced it with a queen-sized mattress for Elvis to lounge on.

"He was such a lover, such a sweet soul. No matter what he needed, we made sure he had it. Hip surgery, whatever. He slept with me and Claudia his entire life. He slept sideways, he was a bed hog, and he snored, but still so sweet.

"We have a new mastiff, Thor, who is really a dog. He loved puppy class and loves the dog park. He's very social, he is all about mixing it up; he has a lot of personality.

"Dogs show you every day how much they love you. I can be gone a couple hours or just down to the garage for a couple minutes, but either way, the welcome is like, 'Oh man, I love you.' Our pets are part of the family. You honor them in that spirit."

Little Jimmy Dickens

"If you love'em, they'll love you back. I've been around animals all my life, and I've noticed that their moods come along with yours. If you're in a good mood, they know it. If you're in a bad mood, they know it. If you're sick, they know it. They just tune in.

"All my animals have different personalities. Lucy is a big sweetheart. DJ is so smart, he knows when you have something for him and he'll go crazy 'til he gets it. Fred is just plain a character, and Katie plays mean but there isn't really a mean bone in her body.

"These animals mean almost as much to us as our own children, because they become a part of you as time goes by. They soothe my soul, I can honestly say that.

"We spend all our spare time out here in this garden, it's our little haven. The animals love it and we can be out here with all four cats and the four dogs, and really have some fun. The dogs get to singing (barking) and it's like four-part harmony. We love it, and we wouldn't have it any other way. We have a pet cemetery in this garden, in loving memory of our cat Morris, who has been gone for seventeen years.

"We've rescued and we've nursed quite a few cats and we really love them a lot. We have seventeen-year-old Casper and nineteen-year-old Killer. We found Muffie in a parking lot. Tigger we adopted from Happy Tails; she's a beauty. We have rescued, we have adopted and our animals are part of us, even our fish, and we name every last one.

"Love on'em, just love on'em—it's good for the heart."

Joe Diffie

"**L**obo, Tinker, and Little Bit . . . I just love them. Lobo came with my marriage to Theresa, then she found Tinker, and I thought we were done with having dog children, but then she brought home Little Bit.

"What a great feeling it is, to have these little creatures who love you so much. You can lose some of your frustrations and upset emotions just by petting them. It relieves some of that tension that ya have, the way they love to cuddle and hang out with you. When I watch TV at night, Tinker will jump up on my shoulder and sit there. Joy, comfort, and love—there is a real reason pets are here for us. We'll always have one; it just completes the household.

"I'm proud to say that my wife, Theresa, has dedicated a large part of her life to animals and our pets. Please, everyone, spay and neuter. Have a strong sense of responsibility before you commit to a pet."

Crystal Gayle

"They give their love to us. I have a lot of friends who have animals for companionship. They are good companions; they are so sweet. My cat just loves to talk to me. We have conversations.

"I have had cats and dogs all my life, along with horses and chickens. Pets have always been important to me, and since I'm gone a lot, these funny little characters fill a void for my children. I've watched our dog, Rosie, be such a good mother and I admire her so. She's remarkable!

"Our daughter has had a big role in helping with our animals. Some have been challenged and she has been right there helping to take care of them. I am glad that my children have taken the time to be a part of our animals' lives. We've all learned a more loving, giving life because of these sweet, living beings."

Brandon Giles

"I got Beatrice from an old lady who lived up on a mountain back in the woods. She ran a moonshine still for a living. It was a long ride on lots of dirt roads, and the lady had two kittens. One had been born with a broken leg and had a little white cast on its back leg. She was keeping that one, so I took the other one. I named her Beatrice Boogie-leg. The lady told me that she was a 'magic cat.'

"You know, love transcends human relationships. It is just as strong between animals and people. Beatrice makes me laugh out loud every day. She talks back when I talk to her. When I play the piano and sing and then I stop, she looks at me and shakes her head and screams. I can't figure out if she's glad the song is done, or if it's an enthusiastic cheer. It's probably not the latter.

"She's an inside cat, and right now it's the busy time of the year with her job. She's the "bug patrol" and it's ladybug season, so she's always looking up. Beatrice believes that I'm the pet and she's the boss.

"A lady once told Billy Graham that she had never been married and that all she'd had was her beloved dog. When her dog died, she was so depressed and upset, she asked him if her dog would be in heaven waiting for her. He quoted a Bible verse to her that stated that heaven was a perfect place where she would have perfect peace and happiness. If she could not have perfect peace and happiness without her dog, then her dog would most certainly be there, waiting. Made sense to me.

"I think Beatrice is glad that she picked me. I'm glad, too, because I've always wanted a 'magic cat.'"

Vince Gill

"I've had dogs all my life. Now it's kids. Dogs, kids, dogs, we like it that way. There is a real special distinction about the harmony between animals and humans. It's warmness; it's a pure love. I think everyone needs to be a little better tuned into the needs of other living beings, outside our own little worlds.

"Listen, I want this earth to be a better place for my children. I need to be an example. I'm happy to be associated with bettering our community, and if that means speaking out about a topic like animals, who make us all happy and change so many lives, that's the easy part. If we can convince people to adopt, we can really make a difference and lighten the load at these shelters. Please, extend your hearts."

Andy Griggs

"Every animal offers you a different side of love. Especially dogs. Every class of dog is like a denomination of church.

"A bluetick hound is a lazy, 'I love ya, I may not get up and greet ya, I'm way too tired, but look at my face and know that I missed ya' kind of love. Whether they're laid out on the floor or out in the woods hunting, I can't help but love 'em. They are honestly all nose and ears and no brains. I'll be sweeping and they don't even have the sense to get up; they just barely roll over. Oh, every day I have a different story. Some days they don't have the sense to come out of the rain. It makes me love them even more.

"We have a bond, and that bond is hunting. They get so excited about it, they would hunt all night if I wanted them to. That is about the only time I get any action out of them. Come back to the house, and they're gonna sleep twenty, twenty-four hours. But put the leash on them, take them to the woods, and they will run and run and run. That is what they are passionate about; raccoons and me, that's what they love.

"I think that a bluetick is probably the most lonesome-sounding dog there is. I wish I could get them to moan for y'all. When they start running and they get way off, they sound like a train in the distance. Delila, she has the lowest voice, she's the bass singer. Samson is the baritone singer. I'll hear Samson light up under Lila and they get that harmony going. That is why their registered name is 'Andy's lovesick blues.' Their sound is something somewhere between a train and an old Hank song. When I hear them, it is all about the music.

"There isn't much in life that is as faithful a companion as a dog, so I honor that. Sure, there are things in life that are more important than animals, but not a lot. You can never ask for a better friend. Treat them like one. Dogs are no different than friends or family. These dogs will follow me to the ends of this earth, and I would do the same for them."

The Haggar Twins

Jimmy Haggar

"**M**y dog, Winston, was on death row at the shelter. He'd been in and out of hospitals, back and forth to the shelter, and a good old friend brought him over to my house because he had been deemed unadoptable. My friend thought that he was perfect for me but I was hesitant at first, I must admit. I tried frantically to find a home for him, but he started growing on me, ya know? I could not see him go down, so I kept him. I hoped he'd get well, but he didn't. He didn't last long, but I loved him and I was there for him for as long as I could be. When we said good-bye, he wagged his tail.

"Now there's Jack. He was sitting in front of a Kroger, filthy dirty with a broken leg, severe burns, and fleas. He feared everyone except me. He's a babe catcher. He is a total lover boy. Absolute heaven. These animals have meant so much to me. They don't form an opinion. They're always trying. The smiles, the wags, it's like medicine. He loves me. We have a connection and I know it. I'm getting old, and I need companionship. I've always had animals in my life. Character is everything in life, and they add character and then some. They rule!"

In loving memory of Winston.

Ty Herndon

"I love my dogs. We got Jake, when he was a month old; we rescued him from people who were moving. Jake's a little slow. We got Cowboy when he was six months old. They love living in the Hollywood Hills. I live on a circle and we trained them to run around it, so we'll look out the window from time to time and see them go by. It's pretty funny, 'cause they think they're on a big adventure.

"One of my very best friends died of cancer. When I got the news I was sitting on the end of my bed, and I lost it. Cowboy jumped up on the bed, put his head in my lap, and did not leave for three hours. He stayed right

there until I got out of bed and then followed me around for two days, right by my side. I don't know what I would have done without him. Then Jake got in on the action—being a little slow, there was a two-day delay. He'd come up and put his cold little nose on my arm to let me know he was there, as if to say, 'I'm prayin' for ya,' and then scurry off. But Cowboy stood vigil.

"When I come home, they just jump all over me. They make home, home. Saturday and Sunday are our big days at the park, and every night we do the big circle a couple times.

"I wish we could all love each other like pets love us. It's like a child's love, a lot of good energy. These creatures are gifts from our higher power. You have to open up your eyes and receive these gifts, otherwise you'll sit around all your life looking at wrapped gifts. I've started unwrapping mine. There are some amazing things in those boxes when you start opening them."

Rebecca Lynn Howard

"**M**y husband got Trixie for me, because I didn't have any family in Tennessee. She became my instant family and I am absolutely head over heels in love with her. She sleeps with me at night, under the covers in the crook behind my knees. If she gets hot, she'll work her way out and lay her head on the pillow. She doesn't know she's a dog, so please don't tell her. She's so kind to everybody; she likes being around people; she's real playful and fun. I think we're a lot alike that way.

"When I get my guitar out, she'll stick her nose right in the strings. She loves the banjo, too. It's so weird; she knows when my video comes on CMT. I don't know if she recognizes my face or the sound, but every time my video comes on, she races to the TV as if to say, 'Where's the sound coming from? You're sitting right there.' She knows her momma, but when she's around my husband, Jason, she knows he's the protector, so she never barks. It's like she hands that role over to him.

"We love this animal so much and we just want everyone to consider adopting a dog before going to a pet shop. There are so many wonderful dogs in the shelters and on the street that need homes. My brother-in-law has adopted two and they are the sweetest, kindest, most grateful dogs in the world. How could anyone abuse a pet? They're like your kid. Trixie and I know each other inside out! When I look in her eyes, she takes all the burden of stress off my soul."

Brett James

"Oh, this cat and I have a very special connection. Buster's been in my life for a very long time and we understand each other very well. I have a big family and I love it that way, but when I'm gone he's not too much for my wife to take care of. He's cool that way. He's cool period! He was a rescue and I know for a fact that he's very happy to be where he is now.

"We went to the shelter, and he jumped in our arms. We knew he was the one. He was the most spoiled cat in the whole world, before kids. It is a different life now with four children, but as soon as I sit down he's in my lap, and as soon as I finish a bowl of cereal, he's waiting to drink the milk off the bottom of my bowl. He's so great with the kids, especially our six-month-old. He just likes to cuddle up and be a friend. As soon as the kids are in my lap, he is, too. He's very protective of them, as well. He's like their uncle, Uncle Buster.

"I think everyone should adopt or rescue—it's good for the soul, and listen, you've saved a life. If just a small percentage of the population were to adopt and take care of an animal by spaying and neutering, just think how dramatically we could cut down on the number of homeless pets. Animals are such a gift from God—and God's creatures should be honored."

George Jones

"Bandit is our baby girl. She was given to me by our daughter, Sherry, for my birthday. She was a surprise, a big surprise. I named her Bandit after my record label. She's crazy about my wife, Nancy, and me. Bandit follows us everywhere; she can really get up under your feet sometimes, too. Oh, she just wants to be right there. You can't get mad at her 'cause she's just telling you how much she loves you. I don't know who she loves more, me or Nancy.

"Every morning when we wake up, Bandit and I walk down to the gate and back. That's our morning ritual. Then we get on the golf cart together and cruise around our property. She loves sittin' up and lookin' at everything, like she's in charge. She follows the sun. Where there's a warm, sunny spot, there's Bandit. It's the same when she's in the bus, too—she's either in the window watching or sunning herself. When she hears the garage door open when I come home, she races to the door and if she can make it out in time, she'll jump right in the car to welcome me home.

"She's always right there for Nancy and me. She lives to love us. I guess you could say that she gives the same amount of love that you would want to receive, and for us, that's a whole lot!"

Cledus T. Judd

"I've always had pets. The first pets I had as a little boy were a Pekingese and a duck. You'd never see the dog without the duck or the duck without the dog, or them without me around. We were big pals. One day the duck ran off and the dog went looking for him, and I never saw either one of 'em again. I guess you can say it was a real love story. You can get incredibly attached to them. It was hard to function there for a couple of weeks, especially as a kid, 'cause there was such an innocent passion. You can get so attached to them, sometimes overly. Then you suffer when something happens.

"Love them while you got 'em. They need to be nurtured and held, talked to, and got onto and scolded. They're not really sure when and what they do wrong, just like a kid. So I think every once in a while you gotta remind them who's the boss. But for the most part, it's all about the nurturing. For all the love you give 'em, they'll definitely give it back.

"Now I've got a pug and a poodle—that's what happens when you've got a girl in your life. You can tell when pets are in love with you, you can tell when they're mad at you; they have emotions, too. They can get on your nerves, barking and clawing and chewing on something, and then they look at you, tryin' to say they're sorry or they love you. Well, I just fall apart. They just make your knees buckle. It's a cool feeling and they win every time.

"Sometimes I just wish they could talk. What would they say? I'm hungry; I love you; who knows? We do the talkin' for 'um. Dogs can do the craziest things to grown men. You take the most macho, hulkster kind of guy with a big ol' gruff voice, and the minute he gets around them, it's 'Come here, little Boo Boo.' Dogs definitely win every time."

The Kinleys

"We have rescued about fifty animals and happily placed them in great homes, thank goodness. All of our pets are rescued, spayed or neutered, and we promote that at all our concerts.

"Animals teach us how fragile life is, how one little spirit can mean so much. If you disregard that innocent spirit, it's like discarding a part of yourself, and we want to do everything in our power to help neglected animals everywhere. Once, when we were on vacation, a dog was following us from place to place. We snuck him into our hotel room, bought him an airline ticket, and brought him home to Nashville, mange, parasites, and all. Papi now has a wonderful home here in America."

"It's all about respect for life and sharing the life we treasure. If we can convince everyone to extend their hearts and their homes, and educate their children, we can all experience the love of a pet. Now, that's living!"

Tracy Lawrence

"I've got all kinds of animals—horses, cows, dogs, and cats. A full cast of characters from the barnyard to the front yard. This big ol' Rot is a lover; she's a good'n. She's been around a long time. The crazy bulldog's just like a temperamental artist. She stays in her crate and acts like she is scared of the world, but when it's show time (play time) she comes dashing out as if to say, 'Hey, I wanna play, too!' Sorta like Tanya Tucker—she may be a little late comin' on stage, but when she shows up, she shows up! I love you, Tanya!

"Well, the horses are part of my soul. When I come home and I've got my kids and my wife and my animals, I really feel I'm home. It's the peace of harmony, and no busy schedule can take that away from you. Yeah, I'm blessed and I'm happy. And I'm positive these animals have a big, big part in that."

Shannon Lawson

"We have two dogs. Galileo is our Great Dane, and our newer addition is Gracie. We used to have this little dog named Pacco, who was hilarious; Galileo used to swing him around by his collar. When I was on the road, Pacco got out and got hit by a car. We were devastated.

"Some weeks later, my wife, Mandy, went to the Humane Society and found Gracie. She was so funny lookin', with a big ol' head. She has been the biggest blessing. Smart as a whip. If you tell her to stay in the yard and watch our baby, River, she'll do it. She checks on the baby constantly.

"I had tons of dogs growing up and they have always kept me grounded. Life can be difficult, but they make it simple. She shows so much respect to my wife and me. She understands the connection. Her role is somewhat of a protector. They have little souls, like we do. They are here to teach us. Very spiritual!"

Brenda Lee

"I've been an animal lover all my life, and, since my children were little, we've never been without a slew of well-loved family pets—even 'adopted' neighborhood strays. No matter, each forever became a bona fide member of the family. There was Major Jack, Bernie, Little Bit, Stanley, Sassy, Kobe, Fritz, and Midget, and, mindless of the breed, size or pedigree, we'd inevitably nickname each one Buddy. They were truly our buddies and our pals.

"As the years passed and as life would have it, I've cried over each one and sadly said goodbye when I lost them, primarily due to illnesses. That's why, after such a heart-breaking loss about ten years ago, I vowed to never have a dog again. Nevertheless and soon after, my youngest daughter surprised me with a Rottweiler puppy on my birthday. I decided right then and there that he was my 'Buddy' through and through.

"Every day over the years, Buddy would look at me with grateful eyes. His greatest joy would be when I walked in the room. Part big and clumsy.

Part very protective. All affection, devotion, and acceptance. Always a presence of calmness in the midst of chaos. Expecting nothing in return. Faithful to the end.

"That's why this particular photograph is special. In loving memory of my dear pet Buddy, who died last year after almost ten years of unconditional love and protection, I pose here with Buddy's father, Rutger."

Danni Leigh

"Kat, my cat, came from the Humane Society in Florida. I was packed and ready to move to Nashville and my boxer was going to be staying with my boyfriend. I'm so attached to my animals. I couldn't imagine not having a pet to come home to in a new city, a new apartment, so I was thrilled to get Kat. She was just a little kitty and we were attached at the hip right from the start.

"I got a job when I first moved to Nashville working for Dixie and Tom T. Hall, working out on their farm with all their animals. One day, at the vet, they said, 'You have to see this dog that came in; you just have to take him; he's unbelievable.' So I did. Everyone fell in love with him overnight and they named him Petey, because he looked like Petey from the Little Rascals. He's the only dog I know that likes the vet, because he lived there for a month before he could actually come home with me. He got so spoiled.

"Then there's Samson. Lots of fans knew about me having had a boxer that I'd had to leave with his dad when I moved. I had gone to Florida to do a show during Biketoberfest, and this family of breeders showed up with a basket of Boxer puppies and gave me one. I called my best friend, who animal-sat for me when I was on the road, and she said to bring him home, so we added Samson to the family!

"These animals are the loves of my life. They know when I'm sick or when I am happy, and they make me feel so good. I love the chaos and the mayhem when I come in the door—'Hey, Mom's home!' I live for it. I love it.

"I also have a sugar glider, Chloe. She's a marsupial. They're like squirrels and they're nocturnal, so they're perfect for a musician. She's so small that I can take her anywhere.

"Pets have such different personalities, and when you look into their eyes, you realize that they have emotions. If a person would take time to understand that, he could never harm or disrespect an animal in any way."

Little Texas

Del Gray

"When my wife and I moved into our lake house out in Henderson we had this big, fenced-in yard, and I'm thinkin', 'I grew up with dobermans and boxers, I'm gonna get me a manly dog!' Well, my wife says, 'I grew up with small poodles,' and I'm thinkin', 'Oh, man, I *gotta* have a manly dog.'

"A friend of my dad's had a standard poodle when I was growing up and he was a really smart dog, so I started calling around and found a breeder in Chattanooga. I told her I wanted the biggest white poodle she had. She said that she had a twelve-week-old that was already twenty pounds, and I said, 'That's my dog.' We drove to Chattanooga and picked up Alex. We had to wash our hands, take off our shoes, and answer twenty questions before we could take him home.

"Six months later we got Abbey, a sixty-pound black female. She is the hellion. She'll take the frozen chicken out of the sink and tear into it. When we get home, Alex will be sitting on the couch with the 'I didn't do it' look on his face. Abbey will walk up with her tail tucked between her legs and give us the 'I'm sorry' look, like she can't help herself.

"Our dogs are like our kids. Abbey is the kind who will love when she needs it, but Alex will put his head on your shoulder as if to say, 'Dad, I'm so glad you love me.' They are such good listeners and they are very, very smart.

"Abbey loves it when I play the guitar; she'll sit by me on the sofa and I'll sing to her. She's one of the fans who accepts my singing for what it is. Alex is a drum dog—when I play, he sits on the couch and he seems so proud of me. They are both so connected to music.

"They are our world. We actually bought our dogs a camper so that we could travel with them. I know they love me. We're good together."

Barbara Mandrell

"I have been an animal lover all my life. I am never too busy to stop and lend a helping hand to God's creatures, both great and small. I've got cats, dogs, a cockatoo, and a thirty-gallon tank of fish. Dandy Lion, our yellow Lab, was a gift from a friend to our son, Nathan. Boomer, our late black Lab, saved Dandy Lion's life. Boomer was barking wildly at the door and I'm so intensely tuned in to these animals, I knew there was something very wrong. I opened the door and Boomer took off running. I followed him to the creek, where we found Dandy Lion going down for what may have been the last time if Boomer hadn't heard the pup's cry. Needless to say, there was a deep, loving bond there.

"Cheetah's Den, a Bengal cat, I refer to as Kumate (which is Japanese for fight to the death). She's a one-person cat. Ken, my husband, gave her to me on Valentine's Day. I believe God gave us dogs and cats to love us. This is the only life they get, and we are responsible for making it a good life."

Louise Mandrell

"These dogs are rescues, but I got them from someone who sells Chinese cresteds. One was abused before I got her; the other was a baby. Another, the breeder was concerned about her health. She had actually been sold and I asked if the purchaser could afford all the medical bills to keep her alive, and, well, now I have her.

"These dogs go to work with me every day. When they demand my attention I stop and play with them. Sally will bring me a toy and Emily will go over to the treat door and just throw a fit. I'm so busy all the time, they make me stop working long enough to pay attention to them, and that's good for me

"I've used my dogs as an example to the men in my life. What I tell them is, you will learn from the girls. Number one, they bark because they want you to pay attention to them. Number two, they gruffle if you don't pay attention to them. And number three, they'll bite you if you don't pay attention to them. They will get that mad if you don't stop and pet them! So, my girls teach the men in my life how to treat the girls in their life.

"As an entertainer, I have found it easy to place pets. I do it from the church services I have every Sunday at my theater in Pigeon Forge. One time I went out to the congregation and said, 'Would you feed Louise Mandrell if she was hungry?' and a thousand people loudly said, 'Yes.' I asked, 'If Louise Mandrell was to love you unconditionally, would you take her home with you?' Everyone said yes again. So I said, 'Just a minute,' and I went and got the dog, brought her out with me, and I said, 'I would like everyone to meet Louise Mandrell.' She'd been named after me, and a lovely doctor and his wife and their child took Louise home.

"I need lots of people in my life, and I do two to three shows a day because I love people. I love animals just as much. Because of the career I've chosen I'm not with my family all the time, and the animals have become a part of my family. They fulfill my need to be needed."

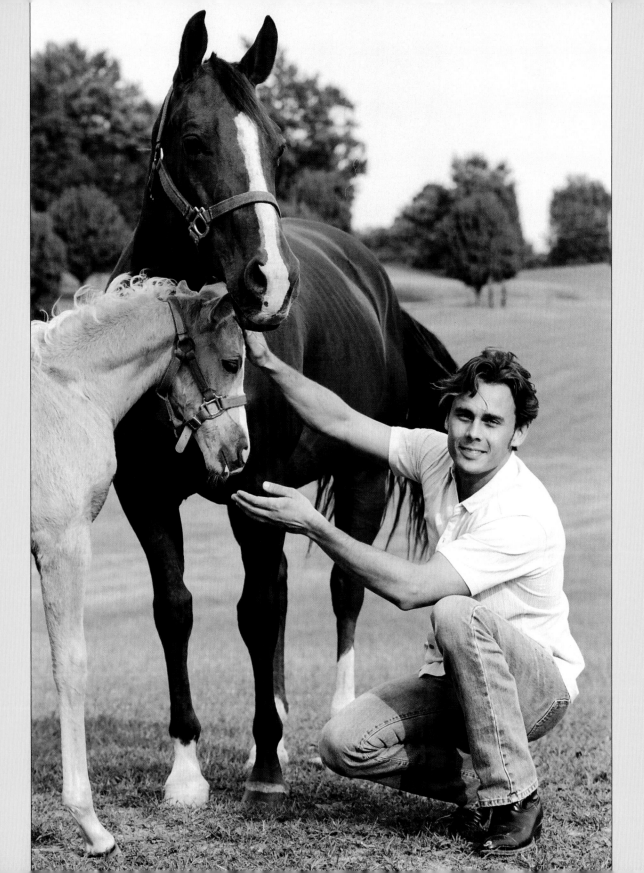

Brad Martin

"I grew up around animals. I remember coming home from school and they'd always be there, very comforting. No matter what's going on in your life as a kid or an adult, you can confide in an animal. You can get comfort and a release from every hard aspect of your life from them. They are very nurturing; you give love to them and they give back that same affection. So animals mean a lot to me.

"There is life there that needs to be nurtured and respected. They cannot live without our help—how precious that is.

"These wonderful dogs are my friends. I don't have a pet right now because I'm traveling so much, but when I can, I'm gonna go straight to the shelter. When I'm ready I'll know 'em when I see 'em!"

Mila Mason

"I got Samantha while I was at a fishing tournament with Tracy Byrd, for his charity. She had these tricks that she does; I guess she learned them for survival. People kept giving her food and she was literally begging for someone to take her home; she kept jumping on the boat. Evidently she had been dumped with a load of puppies at the convenience store. I fell for her. So I took her home and on the ride she crashed; she was exhausted from begging. Hey, begging takes a lot of energy! I think she slept for days after that.

"These animals just surprise me every day. When I brought my baby home, they became nannies. They would come get me when the baby would wake up. They watched over her, they would kiss her goodnight. They don't care about anything except for love. If you've ever had a lonely day in your life and you're just a mess, they are so sensitive and so in-tune, it's amazing. Their family is everything to them. They wait for us to come home, their little faces in the windows like children.

"It is addictive, their love, and we should all have it in our hearts to love animals. I do measure people as to whether or not they like animals. If they don't, it is a sure shot that I probably won't like them.

"I think the human race is such a kind race that if people really knew what was going on around them in the shelters, knew about the loss of lives, they would be heartbroken. When I found out, I couldn't even comprehend it. I hope we can raise awareness. If everyone made a contribution, no matter how small, toward spaying and neutering, this world would be a better place—and maybe, just maybe, it would make a difference in everyone's lives."

Neal McCoy

"We researched these dogs on the Internet. My wife started looking and we found a breeder in Austin. We wanted a big dog, and I think she found about the biggest one there was! While we were doing a show down at a rodeo in Austin, my wife chose the puppy. We loved his markings and we thought he was so beautiful, and thought he'd turn into a nice dog.

"Dogs just love you no matter what you do. You can get onto 'em, or scold 'em, or hug 'em, but no matter what, they keep lovin' you. They are just so loyal. We've had cats, too, but cats are a whole different animal. Cats *allow* you to have them. Dogs actually love you back. Being there, just being there; that's what I love about a dog—just like my family members. When I come off the road, I expect to see my family and my dog. I love getting out in the yard and tootin' around together, wrestlin' and playin'!

"Animals cannot take care of themselves. They may do okay out in the wild for a little while, but as a rule, they depend on us to be fed, sheltered, and taken care of when they're sick. There are a lot of pet lovers out there, and I'm one of them. We can only hope and pray that people will do the right thing."

Jo Dee Messina

"I fell in love with Russell at first sight. I was working in California and I drove by the 'Puppies' pet store and he looked at me and I at him. I sent a runner from the venue back to get him, in a panic for fear he'd been sold. I had to have him, I just had to have him!

"He's really spoiled. He follows me around everywhere. He has an awesome personality. He plays fetch with himself, and it cracks me up. I love watching him. I think he takes after his Mom, he is silly and loves acting silly. He'll take a bone and he'll whip it across the room, then he'll kick it, like he doesn't know where it's going. He does that with the ball, too. He really is like his Mom; he is an entertainer.

"When I am playing the piano, he'll just lay at my feet. I know it's louder down there but he doesn't care, just as long as he's with me. He's been raised on the road and goes everywhere with me, so the crew and everybody knows Russell.

"Animals help us out in so many ways, they always have. You must love them and show them that they are appreciated. They have feelings, too. Animals have helped us work for centuries. There are Seeing Eye dogs, dogs that help the hearing impaired, and they help people who are physically challenged. Dogs even assist in rehabilitation. It is unreal what dogs can be to people.

"If kids can show compassion for an animal and responsibility, that helps to develop their compassion as an adult. People who dump an animal have no compassion in their soul. I have a few rescues, in addition to Russell, so I know. It is sad that some people have no tenderness in their soul.

"They give us so much, they add so much to our lives; they have such a pure and innocent need, such a pure and innocent goal. They don't want your money, they don't want to trick you. All they want is your love. It is pure, simple, and genuine."

Dean Miller

"They give you everything, where love is concerned. They never reject you; they're always open. All you have to do is provide them with food and a place to live, and they love you, love you, love you, like you've given them the world. They make no demands on you; they just give and give more. Their hearts aren't convoluted and complex, like humans' hearts.

"They have as great a capacity for emotion as we do, if not more. We should always be aware of that and their extremely sensitive emotions. There are times when people let you down, but animals never do."

Montgomery Gentry

Eddie Montgomery

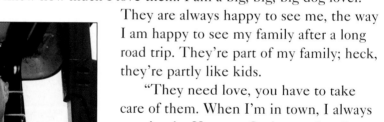

"I have always been a big animal lover, period. When I come home I just love hangin' with 'em, especially when I go fishin', or goin' around the farm. I know they are always there. If I go into town they are right there in the back of my truck. I have a lot of fun with them and so do my kids. I reckon when it comes down to it, everybody has some kind of stress factor, but my dogs don't, they're livin' life and havin' fun. Sometimes I wish I could be more like them—laid back, go huntin' whenever I wanted to.

"My dogs know how much I love them. I am a big, big, big dog lover. They are always happy to see me, the way I am happy to see my family after a long road trip. They're part of my family; heck, they're partly like kids.

"They need love, you have to take care of them. When I'm in town, I always stop by the Humane Society and walk through and visit the animals. If I was home more, there is no telling what-all we would have out here.

"I got these two cats from the Humane Society. I was havin' a problem with mice back at our barn and after I got the cats, I discovered that the mice were disappearing. They've got the run of the place, they have their own door, they can go in and out. Ah, hell, I love 'em all!"

Allison Moorer

"Henry is a Humane Society cat. We had just gotten our first cat, Wanda, and decided she needed some company. We walked in, spotted Henry in a cage all by himself, and decided he was the one for us. He was older than most of the other kittens, and was unique looking—more blond than yellow.

"I love all kinds of animals and I'd adopt them all if I could! Henry is one of the most loving animals I've ever had. Sometimes he scratches on the furniture or screams at the bedroom door, but when he's being sweet, it's the best. He loves to sit in my lap when I'm answering e-mails, and loves to play with Nocoma, fur, mice, and shoestrings.

"Pets pick up on what's going on. They go through moods just like people do, and we should pay close attention. I'm thankful that we've been able to give our cats good, safe, comfortable lives. There are so many out there without good homes and I'm glad our three have a nice place to grow!"

Lorrie Morgan

"I cannot imagine life without dogs. I love animals and I've had as many as six at one time. There is just something about a dog that calms you.

"I bought my German shepherd, Punky, on the side of the road for twenty dollars, and I bought a golden retriever for my husband, Sammy. I am crazy about my papillons, Elvis and Marilyn; they are so smart and quick. They are living with my daughter Morgan now, but they're family for as long as we are blessed to have them.

"I really get upset when I see something on the news about animal abuse and neglect. It's like having children: if you can't feed them and take care of them, then don't get pregnant. The same goes for animals—if you aren't going to take care of a pet, don't get one.

"I've been tempted a couple of times to pick up dogs just 'cause they didn't look happy. So if your dog is missing, I probably got 'em!"

Jonell Mosser

"I married into Macy, my palomino. She was my husband's but we bonded quickly. She is sweetness and patience, a real darling. We're into performance horses, and we have twenty-five. We also have a new dog that someone dropped off here at the farm. We named him Bene, which means *good* in Italian, because we want him to be all that goodness brings. We also have a barn cat named Oliver. He keeps the mouse population down and he's a real sweetie, too.

"An animal's love is for a lifetime, and you know that when you look at them. It makes me want to be better than my species. To find something more eternal in the center of my being, rather than the outside.

"When I'm with them, I can just lean my head up against them and they give me a sense of peace and a moment of calm. Everything else is gone, and it's just me and the animal. I focus on them and they on me. You can't put a value on moments like that.

"If you show by example how to treat animals and people better, hopefully people will learn from that. It is an ever-evolving process."

The Oak Ridge Boys

Joe Bonsall

"We've got nine cats. I love them. I've written children's books about Molly (the Molly the Cat series), then there's Omaha, Sally Ann, Gypsy, Ted, Baybe, then some outdoor cats. They each have a story, of course. I was on the road in Omaha, Nebraska, and my wife and I saw "Omaha" and fell in love, so we bought her. Molly was brought to our front door by my nephew. Sally Ann and I met at an Oklahoma book signing that was done in association with the local Humane Society. We found Ted when we were driving up by our farm and saw these abandoned kittens. So we scooped them up and had them spayed and neutered, and we kept Ted. Baybe, she was dumped off at the front door. Bud was a neighbor's cat—he was over here all the time, so the neighbor just brought the papers over one day.

"The incredible thing to me about these cats is that all of them are so different. Like people, each and every one has its own personality. The one thing they have in common is that they're all very loving.

"My wife, Mary, was the one who really taught me about love, and she was the one who introduced me to cats. I kind of feel like Hemingway now: 'A house may be a home without a cat, but how can it prove its worth?' I think a cat or dog in the house just makes everything more beautiful. Pets are a long-term commitment, and Mary and I started a foundation that promotes responsible pet ownership.

"A guy has to know his place in a house like mine. Every time we get a new cat, I drop one more rung on the ladder. It's okay; I can handle it. If my wife isn't home, they all come and lay around me, but if she's home, I'm in last place. They give you companionship, love—and besides that, a cat is the most beautiful creature in the world; they are like art! Elegant! They are the energy force of our house."

K.T. Oslin

"Mabel, God love her, is a rescue. There was this guy who was one of these bad breeders and my vet took some puppies away from him. Mabel was almost dead, and it took the vet two months to nurse her back. My vet tried to convince me to take her and no sooner did I say, 'I don't want a dog,' then I said, 'Oh, bring her over.' Poor, terrified little Mabel—she was a piece of work. It took me about two years to get her half straightened out. I almost gave her away a couple of times, and I don't give up. I thought it wasn't a good match, but Mabel has really come around.

"I thank her for teaching me to be extremely patient and logical about how to do things. People either don't give the dog enough credit or they give them way too much, and then they're disappointed when the dog doesn't come through. You need common sense and consistency! I looked at her one day and just said, 'Mabel, we're just gonna do this.' She's four now; it's the magic age. I think all dogs reach four and say, 'Oh, I get it.' It's like they reach their maturity then.

"She is so kind, so sociable, and a fun little dog around other dogs and cats. She's turned out so well. It shows you, dogs are just like people: if you have a bad start you pay a price for it for a while, but if someone will be a little patient and be smart, they almost all come around.

"Mabel and I respect each other's needs. She's an independent little girl so she sleeps in another room, which was hard for me to get used to. She gives me my space, and she reads me pretty good, too. We're a perfect match.

"We have it so easy in this country that we've lost respect for life. If you're going to own pets you have to be sensitive to their needs, or what's the point? Do your research first and foremost, because animals always pay the price. They companion us, they all serve a reason and a purpose, and I just groove on 'em!"

Brad Paisley

"When you have a big animal who looks to you for everything, his health and shelter and all his other needs, it's a huge responsibility. He is so different than the small pets I've owned.

"There is nothing like walking out into this field and having him see me and come to me. He'll do that with anybody that he's getting to know; I bet the next time y'all come out here, he'll come up to the fence. That is a personality trait not all horses have. He is very docile.

"In the Bible it says God created animals and man, and we were given dominion. Some people might see that to mean animals are less important, but I don't see it like that. Knowledge gives us the responsibility of understanding why things happen and of taking care of animals, who don't understand.

"Owning an animal brings you closer to nature and being around animals this size teaches you the order of things. I find it a spiritual experience, frankly, closer to God. Any time you get love, it is a good thing.

"When a kid has a pet, the child learns a lot about commitment. And commitment is a big part of love, because love is a choice."

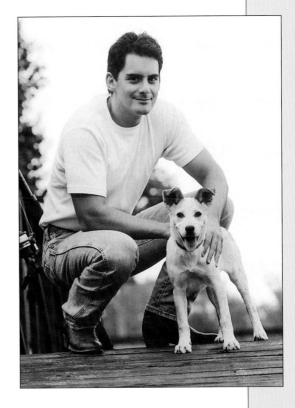

Lee Roy Parnell

"Lillie came from the animal shelter. Her name was actually April at first, but it just didn't work. I couldn't imagine myself walking up and down the neighborhood hollering for April, so I named her after one of my favorite old Bob Wills songs, 'Lillie Dale.' I was crazy about her, but it was clear she had been abused and most likely by a male. To this day, if any man walks into the room, she gets down and barks and looks like she's ready for business. She was like that with me in the beginning. It took a long time to earn her trust, but I always liked her. She's kinda like a kid; you gotta remember that you don't know where they came from or what they've been through.

"The lesson here is that it's worth the effort. Just because somebody is a little rough around the edges doesn't mean there isn't something tender and gentle somewhere inside of them. You've got to be patient enough with them to get to that place. When someone is the hardest to love, that may be when they need it the most.

"Lillie loves the bus. She has her own bunk with her babies. She's great with the band, but if someone comes to the bus that's not in the group, she'll let you know. A great watchdog. She's part Australian shepherd and we're not sure what else, but you can sense a wildness about her. Yet she's so incredibly loving, and you can tell what she likes most is just a lot of love. There is something soothing about caring for and being cared about by an animal. Once you've earned their love, you won't lose it. That's why these animals are so important to us humans.

"After putting two kids through college, I'm grateful that Lillie has no aspirations to go to private school."

Michael Peterson

"My friend Gene found Bubba, my half-chow–half-Akita. He walked by him at the shelter and Bubba gave him the 'You're not gonna leave me here, are ya?' look. So Gene took him home. Well, Gene had to go out of town and asked us to keep him for a few days, which I know now was a trick to give us Bubba on a permanent basis, but we fell in love with him. He's just so fun loving, just a guy's dog. My kids love him, too. I've had a number of dogs all my life but with him it was just an instant connection. He's just a 'Hi, how ya doin',' fun-lovin' kinda dog. Bubba came with his name, though I guess it's a bit of a cliché to be a country singer and have a dog named Bubba.

"Pokey came from a breeder out West. We had a definite interest in Wheatons; my mother-in-law had one. Our breeder friend saw that one pup needed a little extra special care in recovering from a puppy illness; she was a little slow. Hence the name Pokey.

"Both animals have taught me so much about raw love. There is an old saying, 'I just wanna be the kind of person my dog thinks I am.' There is a nugget of truth behind it; dogs are just so loving. No matter what, they are right there for you. But lookin' at the size of Bubba's belly, I think he gets plenty of attention himself! He mows the lawn with me and loves to hang out with me—though he isn't much good at playin' Monopoly.

"Pokey, our AKC champion, has a quiet tenderness, and she's taught me about patience. She's a lot more like my wife, and Bubba is a lot more like me. My dogs are very different, yet I'll see them out in the yard together and I wonder where Bubba would be without Pokey."

Pinmonkey

Chad Jeffers

"I'm single, so I have a fish, Chopper. He's new; I just got him. This is as far as I can go at the moment with commitment to a pet since I am gone so much. Animals deserve day-to-day nurturing. My family has had wonderful pets through the years and I think they teach you as much about love as they do about loss. When a pet dies, it's really like losing a member of the family. It makes you re-analyze your life. I think they teach you to grow up in some ways. Our mom used to always stay on us about feeding the dogs or walking them, and if they had water.

"In your darkest hour, they're still bright and loving."

Michael Reynolds

"I went to the Humane Society with the intention of adopting a dog. Once I was there, I realized I wouldn't be able to take care of a dog the way they should be cared for, so my friend talked me into going into the cat room. The first thing I saw was Miss Eby lying in a basket asleep. I walked over to her and she woke up and those vivid, jade green eyes peered up at me. I immediately fell in love with her and took her home.

"She is just mean as the devil. I think that's why I like her; she's got a little edge to her. At first I thought she didn't like me. Then one day I realized she was following me from room to room, and I thought, maybe she does like me. You just can't judge a book by its cover.

"When I come home at the end of the day, she's here. My apartment used to feel so empty, and she brings it a warm element. She naps with me; we curl up and read a book. But she can be so mean and I'm sure that's why she ended up at the shelter. I'm fairly tolerant. As mean as she can be, I still love her to death. We're the perfect match.

"God is the God of all living things. If we are to respect God, we must respect all his living things."

Rick Schell

"**A**cacia rules the roost. She's a talker, and she'll wake us up in the middle of the night if she's hungry. She wants to be fed and expects it.

"A little over a year and a half ago my mom was dying of ovarian cancer, and we found out that Acacia had cancer within days of that. I said it couldn't happen. She had it everywhere but a year after surgery, she was doing fine. When we took her back to the vet, they thought they were seeing a ghost—they couldn't believe their eyes! She's fifteen now and she's got so much energy.

"Make sure that you get an animal that is suitable to your environment.

She's been perfect for our lifestyle, and we have a person who comes in every day when we're gone. She loves us and she tells us that—like I said, she's a real talker."

Michael Jeffers

"My wife, Karen, has always had Pomeranians. When we met she had a black Pom named Sasha, but she passed away about four to five years into our marriage. Then I started going out on the road and we wanted Karen to have company, so we got Chewy (Chewbaka). Karen's family has Pomeranians, too, and Chewy is an offspring of my brother-in-law's dog. When we're all together, there must be nine to ten Pomeranians.

"Their love is never ending. When I'm gone and I call Karen at night to talk to her, it's comforting to know she has Chewy there. He kisses at night, kisses in the morning, no matter what. When we're all there, it's so much fun. He senses that his family is all together and he's really happy.

"We live at the end of a country road, and we seem to get so many strays; we're always trying to place an animal. There are so many pets, dogs and cats, that need good homes that it just tears me up. We love having animals in our life."

The Ragsdales
Joshua and Shi-Anne Ragsdale

"I've rescued a church bus full of dogs over the last few years, no, really. I found Chaplin, my chocolate Lab, tied to a tree on a six-foot rope. I talked the guy who had him into letting me take him; he'd been tied up for over eight months. Mississippi is a pit bull mix that I actually stole from two guys who were beating him to make him a fight dog. I carried him inside the house and put him in the bed with Shi-Anne and she's had him ever since. If you're around her for any amount of time, you're gonna hear about how much she loves him. Charlie is our Boston terrier mix, who came from the shelter the day after we did the photo shoot for this book. She had been beaten with a hammer; her neck was wrapped with barbed wire, and she had been dragged behind a car for half a mile. I'm not sure how she survived, but she did and she is the sweetest thing on this earth. My heart belongs to KeeKee. She is our fourteen-year-old long-coat Chihuahua that we got when she was six months old. We were her fourth owners, because she's pretty cranky. She was entered in a few dog shows but she would always bite the judges.

"What have I learned from animals? Well, my horse broke my nose and my back, so I'd have to say she taught me how to love painkillers! Dogs have done a much better job. They are a nonstop school of love. One of my first memories is puppy breath on Christmas morning. That is the best, I tell ya. My only complaint is that being around their sweet souls makes it really hard to put up with ignorant people. I'm a hothead with them, and it's my dogs' fault.

"KeeKee has taught me more lessons than any other pet I've had. She's approaching her final years and she's still so feisty. She's also the biggest seven-pound flirt I've ever seen. I love her honesty. When she's hungry, she'll jump in your plate; when she's sleepy, she'll curl up next to you, close her little brown eyes, and let out a big sigh. Without a doubt, my pets have taught me not to do anything half-hearted. Be passionate. Get your money's worth, whether you're chasing a car or having your back scratched.

"My first dog, Aymme, was like a guardian to me. My favorite picture of us is when I was about six, standing in the gravel driveway in just my underwear and rubber boots shooting my b.b. gun at some poor bird. She saw me through a lot of fazes. My lab, Chaplin, is my son. He sleeps in the bed with me on his own pillow and has his own bowl of cereal with me in the morning. Now Shi-Anne has taken the son thing to a new level with Sippi. They are our kids; we relate to them more than we do our relatives.

"I have a Jeep Wrangler, so in the summertime I let the top down and take all the dogs for a ride through the hills. We always stop off at Sonic for supper. Chaplin and Sippi sit in the back, and I toss them tater-tots after they cool down. Charlie likes to ride in my lap or on my shoulder. KeeKee usually shakes because she thinks she's going to the vet, but when she smells the food she perks right up. On Easter Sunday, we hide peanut M&Ms in the yard for them to find. Basically, we treat them how we dream of being treated!

"Take great care of your pets and don't be afraid to stand up to anybody who doesn't treat an animal properly. Also, understand that you can't save all the unwanted animals in the world. I would have a thousand dogs if I could, but you can only take care of so many pets. I look at it this way: every time I feed my dogs, I'm still in the process of rescuing them."

Rascal Flatts

Jay Demarcus

"I adopted Abby from a friend who was leaving town and couldn't take her along with him. I got her at six months and she is one of my true loves. I grew up with dogs, I've had them all my life, and golden retrievers are the gentlest animals in the world. The love I get from this animal is constant and consistent. You can be in the worst mood and they're still thrilled to see you.

"You can find the kind of companionship in a dog that you'll never find in a human being. These animals are put into our lives to be such a source of joy.

"Always remember: dogs don't have to be your friend, they chose to, and they love unconditionally. And that's a great thing to have in your life."

Eddy Raven

"We've got nine dogs; they are a big part of our life. Dingo and Sheba came from a friend of mine in Arkansas, and Toto came from Texas. He was the runt but he's smart, smart, smart. Then we've got four mini pins, an Australian shepherd, and another dog that is half-wolf and half-malamute. We accidentally ran over him in the bus; I didn't see him. He's got three legs, but he doesn't seem to mind. We can't believe he survived and the vet couldn't believe it, either. When I went over to him after I ran over him, he wrapped one leg around me, then took my arm in his mouth so gently, just barely gripping. I knew he wanted to stay on Earth, thank goodness.

"Dogs love for the sake of love. Look, I ran over one. Sure, it was a mistake, but he still loves me. They just give back to you, over and over. Any one of these dogs would die for me. Anytime one is around me, another one is trying to get even closer. When I'm in a chair and I move to another room, they follow me.

"I guess it's like the relationship I had with my brothers and sisters. I'm the oldest of ten and I'm like a big brother to them; when I call, they come to me or they'll argue with me. You can punish them, put 'em outside, but the minute you open that door, it's over. They don't hold any grudges."

"There are some people who are meant to have pets and some that shouldn't. I can't imagine living without them; it's even difficult to leave them. I've built houses in the back for my dogs, with electricity and heat. I like being a dog master; it's a privilege. They are here by the grace of God for all of us. Treat them like you want to be treated because you might be one, one day. I'm a firm believer that the spirit does move around."

Collin Raye

"I lived in Greenville, Texas, and a dear friend had a beautiful German shepherd named Boss that he was going to breed. I've always loved German shepherds and I got the pick of the litter. I picked the one that growled, the one with the spirit—that was Patton. He was so beautiful, and a good size.

"The reason I chose that name is because I am a World War II historian. It was the most horrible time in the history of the world, but in a way it was America's finest time. Patton was one of my heroes; he was aggressive and

had no fear. My Patton took pride in his name; it was as if he knew, because he tried to live up to it every chance he got. So stubborn, so defiant, so brilliant, a great watchdog, so protective. The courage and that heart were eventually what took his life. Having him was a once-in-a-lifetime experience.

"There is no creature that God ever created that is as loyal as a dog. How can we teach humans how to emulate that behavior, and all love one another? What a world we'd live in. I'm a man of faith, and I believe that animals have souls and I will see Patton in heaven again. There was a character and a spirit there. I am sure St. Francis has a great protector. I believe they are part of you forever."

In loving memory of Patton.

Ricochet

Greg Cook

"I have three daughters and we all decided we wanted a dog. So we started looking at Labs and we found Hershey in Kentucky. When we bred Hershey, we kept Mocha out of that litter. Then we found Crochette through a friend. We didn't really mean to get Nestle, but my

buddy wanted me to help him sell her, and I sorta forgot to sell her! They are so different in personality but they all get along. My good friend John Dorris says they'd do anything for ya, all for a pat on the head. Labs want to be a part of your life, no question. They want to be up in your business, no question. You get all that entertainment, just for a pat on the head.

"Labs need you, really need you. The love, the affection, satisfies them. We grill together. My daughters love to walk them, go to the park, and play Frisbee. The dogs just love to love.

"Pets are a full-time commitment; you have to welcome them as part of your family. Don't own a pet unless you are willing to put in the time. I'm in!

"I have so much respect for their natural instincts. It is an honor to learn from them."

Jeannie Seely

"Shadpoke is a term that my mother used. It kinda means little ragamuffin. Whether a kid had a skinned knee or a dog had worms, Mother used to say, 'Poor little Shadpoke.' I hadn't thought about that term in years when a family member called and told me that there was this pitiful abandoned dog in her backyard and that somebody needed to come get him. 'This little guy really, really needs some help,' she said. So I went over and got him. One eye was ulcerated, his fur was badly knotted, and he was absolutely filthy. So I cut back his hair and bathed him, fed him, made him as comfortable as I could that night, and took him straight to the vet the next morning. They operated on his eye, and when I picked him up, they'd shaved him and he was still wobbly from the surgery. I remember looking at him and saying, 'Oh, God love you, you poor little Shadpoke.'

"Dogs have shown me what real love really is. They really listen to you. You know how people are: 'Yeah, I hear ya.' You might hear my voice, but dammit, you don't hear me. Animals want to understand. They're giving you their undivided attention. You don't get that from people.

"I had a friend move to Florida and she had a next-door neighbor who had a shih tzu, a little blond hussy. She was almost three but the owner treated her more like a piece of jewelry than a dog, so I arranged to buy her based on whether Shadpoke liked her. We had a puppy pajama party and we all hit it off. I really didn't buy her; I just paid the lady to let her go. I named her Cheyenne, and she's so good for Shadpoke. He's been more active.

"When people say, 'Animals are just like people,' I say, 'No, they're not.' I wish people *were* more like animals, and had the same open honesty and respect that animals do."

Blake Shelton

"We've got two dogs, Austin and Red. Sound familiar? I was driving my tractor one day and Kaynette was following me in the Gator. The dogs came out of nowhere and jumped right in front of my tractor. They were maybe four or five weeks old at the time. It was a steamy-hot June and the puppies were extremely dehydrated, wormy, and starving to death. We were leaving town that day, going back on the road, so we had to take them with us. They needed to be nursed back to health, so we made many a trip to the vet.

"In return, they have shown us so much loyalty. We're gone so much, but they don't forget. The minute they see our truck, they go crazy. It's amazing how they just know we are their parents. When we are home, we love to squirrel hunt together and they ride on all the farm equipment with me. They are one of the reasons I look forward to coming home.

"It's this simple: Don't get a pet if you don't want one. We feel that our dogs were a gift from a higher power. They were put in our lives for a reason. We took care of their problems, nursed them to good health, and now we have loving, loyal companions. We're the lucky ones!"

Daryle Singletary

"I'm a big George Jones fan, and when we got the yellow Lab, I thought it'd be neat to name him after a legend. So I named him 'No Show Jones.' He don't talk back; you gotta love that. He don't always obey like you'd like, sometimes. But when I'm with him, just him and me in the truck, he's somebody to talk to and he listens to you. He can be stubborn every now and then, like me. He's laid-back like me. I'll have a plate of food and he'll have a bone, and we are both so content. We also have two little kittens.

"I think we take animals for granted. When you sit back and really pay attention, they're so alive. They each have a life, just like a human being, and I think sometimes people lose sight of that. Jones was neutered at seven months because I don't want him going out and making puppies that I can't handle. People need to take that more seriously, to do what we need to do to allow animals a better quality of life. I am a huge supporter of the Humane Society."

Sixwire

Chuck Tilley

"**S**ebastian provides me with lots of happiness, lots of joy. I love teaching him new tricks. Please, folks, love and respect your animals. Please spay and neuter them."

Steve Mandile

"**I** love it when I come home, and these faces are waiting in the window. Emma and Texana never judge you, and that makes it such a joy to come home. They depend on you. I have a very soft spot in my heart for animals. Please dedicate yourself to them."

Robb Houston

"**O**thello and Hamlet are a constant source of companionship for me and my wife. Don't ever get a pet on a lark. Get one only if you really, really want one, then adopt or rescue. It's so important to the community."

John Howard

"**M**aya and Juanita are our babies, and we adore them. They fulfill our every need. Treat them as you would treat yourself. Pets are a healthy addiction."

Andy Childs

"**D**aisy is a member of our family, and she was our firstborn. She is so great with kids; she has a wonderful temperament. You can read dogs' emotions and should try to be intuitive to their needs. Basic care should be obvious, but in case it's not, there are plenty of books. Educate yourself before you take responsibility. It's a big commitment."

Mike Snider

"They've all been teachers to me. I've watched them come and watched them go, each animal has taught me something different. For example, a cat, not unlike a human, will be real nice if they want something. Then once they get what they want, they go on off. Dogs are fun to have around, just like a loyal friend. My kids love dogs also, and since we live in the country we've had several of them. I try to explain that, living in the country, animals don't always survive. I teach my kids to love, enjoy, and take care of our dogs while we have them. However, we must be willing to let them go when it's time for them to move on.

"Our animals have shared with me some very meaningful lessons about life, like to enjoy it as it comes. They are right here, right now, taking care of business. They don't seem to worry about the past or anticipate the future. When my dad lost his favorite dog, he had 'Pure Love' engraved on a little headstone. Unconditional love is the greatest lesson that I've learned from dogs. They accept you as you are. What better lessons can we learn from these little critters than to be as you are and accept all just as it is, right now, without judgment? This is 'Pure Love.'

"This is me and Piper. Ain't he a dandy?"

Sons of the Desert

Drew Womack

"Our cat, Boo, was named after Boo Radley from *To Kill a Mockingbird*. One day he just showed up on our front porch, staring at us. I took the kitten to the vet to get him all checked out, then we made flyers, but nobody claimed him and he became ours.

"My wife had a Chihuahua when I met her, named Punkin. We got another Chihuahua, Peanut, as a puppy. Peanut and Punkin were good friends. Punkin passed away one summer when he was fifteen, and it affected us all deeply. Peanut is still depressed, and I think he's still trying to figure out his role in the family without his friend. He pretends to hate the cat, but we'll catch him playing with the cat. Boo loves Peanut; he thinks he hung the moon. We are pretty sure that the cat thinks he is a Chihuahua, because he was tiny when we brought him in and all he saw was the dogs snuggling under the covers, so he snuggles under the covers. I've never seen a cat do that; he is weird.

"Our pets like a routine, just like us. Peanut doesn't like to wake up before nine in the morning. You have to drag him out, then you have to go back in and find him again. Sometimes it takes a couple minutes to find him. He also loves clean laundry. As soon as my wife takes a load out of the dryer, Peanut is buried in it. And he is right ready for bed when you are. As soon as you get in bed, he is right there beside you.

"It is so important that people understand the responsibility that comes with those cute little faces. People walk into pet stores and say, 'I want that one, right now,' and don't realize they're choosing a lifetime with that animal. They make our lives so rewarding, and it is our responsibility to make their lives just as rewarding."

Jamie Lee Thurston

"Nicole, my ex-girlfriend who is still a friend, wanted a dog, and she found Maka. Nicole was working days and I was performing weekends and writing during the week, so I spent lots of time with Maka. I trained her and we bonded. You need patience, a great deal of patience, but they never give you grief and they can't give you enough love; it's just awesome.

"Growing up, I knew people who would hit their dogs. I would never, never hit a dog. That's not how you get an animal to cooperate or learn. I would take a bullet for my dog; she's probably taught me more about love and life than I'll ever realize. Oh, I miss her dearly. She's in Vermont and I'm in Nashville. When I left, this last trip, she was squeezing, trying to get out through the door to come with me. It ripped my heart out.

"The love I have for her has really taught me how to really care for something else. It teaches you to do for others. How can someone ever take advantage of an animal's loving nature? They are love, pure love.

"I know people who couldn't get along without their pet. If they didn't have their dog as a companion, they just wouldn't make it. That's a strong statement; yep, that pretty much has love written all over it."

Aaron Tippin

"I adopted Buddy from a family in Georgia that couldn't keep him. He learned real quick not to run down the deer and the turkey, that they are not to be chased. He pretty much sticks to the squirrels and rabbits, now.

"Buddy was an only child when he came to the farm. He was a little jealous at first when it came to my daughter, Charla, and my son, Teddy, but he accepted his new family and now he's protective of everyone. He was mesmerized with Teddy as a baby, and really bonded with him as soon as Teddy was old enough to give Buddy a biscuit.

"I was raised in a family that allowed us to have as many animals as we wanted, as long as we were responsible and took care of them.

"God gave us dominion over the animal kingdom, and it is our responsibility to be humane and care for all God's creatures—regardless of who they belong to."

Trick Pony

"Yeah, man, we'd have ten of these shelter puppies travel with us if we could. It's not fair, though. These sweet little guys need a good home; they need to be loved by people who can pay a lot of attention to them and raise them to be good pals to kids. As a group, we feel very strongly about animal adoption. There are so many wonderful little hearts just aching to be loved, and they deserve it. They didn't ask to be brought into this world. Be compassionate. Don't waste money in a prissy puppy shop; go to the shelter! Teach your kids to go for the underdog. He may turn out to be the top dog, with a little extra love and attention. So, from us to you: check your local animal shelter and change your life for the better. Adopt, spay, and neuter."

Tanya Tucker

"I have more dogs than I do children, and I have a couple three of them. That might give ya an idea right there how I feel about animals; I have a big place in my heart for all of them. Not just dogs, either—I've had just about everything. I had my dog Lucy for a long time and I really miss her, but I have quite the cast of characters right here right now.

"I adopted Bella in Colorado. We were traveling through and I was in a guitar store, and I looked up and there was a sign saying that Bella needed a home. Well, I called and told them I'd be leaving town by five. They brought her to my bus at 4:30, and me and Bella, well, we never looked back. Tennessee is her home now. Boy, she can sure run—why, she'll follow me beside the car for about a mile or more, to the edge of my property.

"Now, Tucker just moved in. He showed up one day, we called the name on his tag, and the owner flat out told us that Tucker does his own thing. He started doing his own thing at our house on a regular basis, and we adopted him. A wonderful coincidence, that his name was Tucker. And Pepe is a great little guy; he's real attached to my fiancée. I got him around Eastertime; I just couldn't resist him.

"These dogs are my road buddies. They are so entertaining, I get the biggest kick out of having them on the road with me. I start singing something on the bus, and I look down, and I've got a little audience. They make me smile, they make me laugh, and the kids love 'em, too. It's real clear that every home should have a little critter. It definitely keeps things hoppin'. I'll take them in the bath with me and the kids, and it's one big bubble-bath splash party. They are joy; they have a zest for life—kinda like me.

"Pets are innocent creatures and need protection. Make sure that you teach your kids to take good care of them. If you see something bad going on, report it, don't turn away. Or heck, adopt it yourself. Who knows, maybe you'll end up with one of the best things that ever happened to you in your life!"

Conway Twitty

"We moved to Nashville in the '70s and a boyfriend gave me a dog. I named him ToJo. Some of the neighborhood dogs attacked him and Dad immediately called 911 and ordered an ambulance to come. When they arrived, the medic said, 'Ah, Mr. Twitty, we don't normally do this.' But they helped ToJo, and Dad never forgot it. Daddy treated him just like a family member.

"When my sister, Kathy, was a teenager, she wanted to be actively involved in something to do with animals, so she volunteered at the Sumner County Humane Society, which at the time was a run-down, one-room shack. It had zero money to operate, and what contributions they received were inappropriately used. Kathy came home one day and told Daddy that the conditions were so bad that she couldn't stand it, and something had to be done. Daddy said, 'Honey, let's take a bunch of T-shirts and albums and merchandise, have a sale, and raise some money. I'll donate everything. We'll even ask businesses from the area to donate, too!' They raised enough money to move into a new building.

"At the time, Daddy was organizing celebrity softball games, and he and Barbara Mandrell did an annual softball tournament that benefited the Humane Society. He was so wonderful about being involved in community efforts, raising money, and giving back.

"Daddy was the type who would never hurt another living creature. In fact, when he was older, he would never hunt. As a young man he did strictly for survival. He was the kind of man who would rather pick up a bug and take it outside than kill it. It was God's creation, and he truly valued life."

In loving memory of our father.
We love you, Daddy.
—Michael, Joni, Kathy, and Jimmy

Dan Tyminski

"Columbus is our oldest dog; he's eight. We knew of a breeder who supposedly had wonderful retrievers, so we took a day trip to Harrisburg, Virginia. We only had a choice between the last two puppies in the litter, but I just looked into his face and knew. I knew he'd be a big, healthy boy because the momma and poppa were big. Yeah, we definitely had a connection, but for us it doesn't take much.

"Bones is a newer dog; he came with the farm. He's only been with us a year, but he's been wonderful for Columbus. They are crazy about each other, and they play like puppies. Bones loves running with the horses; they

take off and he tears off after them. He's a little devil; he's the chicken catcher. When we first moved in he attacked one of our chickens, Nanna. She lived in the tack room for a while, convalescing, then we moved the chicken coop into the tree house. Hey, it works!

"Ya know, these animals have taught me that you don't need conditions to love—their love is always there. I wish it were easier for people to love that way. When you're at the end of your rope, no matter what the problem of the day is, you can sit down and talk with a dog, and he'll sit right there and listen.

"I am so grateful for the companionship these animals offer my family. There would be a huge void without them. They deserve our loyalty in return, and I want my children to learn that from me. How better to bring the love full circle!"

The Wilkinsons

"We were looking for a pet that we could take on the bus. We were fascinated by hedgehogs, so we contacted a breeder on the Internet. She brought Piggy to us. Piggy started to get a little plump, and one morning we went in and she had given birth to three baby hedgehogs! We couldn't believe that she had done that all by herself. Immaculate Conception, our little Piggy, ha ha! We were told to wash them and they'd be fine.

"They're the perfect pet. They're especially perfect for musicians because they want to stay up all night and sleep all day. It's so funny; if you get them up too early, they're grouchy. And they eat everything; they're so easy.

"Pets are a huge responsibility, and taking care of those responsibilities is a direct reflection on you as a person. Take the time to do the necessary things for your pet. We will all be happier."

Mark Wills

"When I saw Kirby he had bubble gum all over his legs, and I knew right away—I said that's my dog! Kirby has so much love for my daughters, my wife, and me. He has taught all of us responsibility, and given us so much joy. He's a great kid dog; he's responded very well to a nine-month-old grabbing his ears. And he's so protective: If a stranger comes in the house, he will stand between them and my daughters. He's kinda like the big brother my daughters don't have. And dogs have such a keen sense of your soul. If I've had a bad day, he'll come up and put his head on my lap as if to say it'll be okay. What a wonderful feeling.

"When my wife and I came back from our honeymoon we decided to get a dog, and Kirby was born the day before we got married. Through eating the carpet, running through the screen door, and holes in the wall, we raised our first child, Kirby. It is so satisfying to watch him with our girls and our nephew. Our nephew will sit on Kirby's back and pull his lips around, and Kirby is so patient. He'll go away for a while, and when he's ready he'll come back for more. A pet really needs your love, really needs your care, but gives you so much back in return. The love we offer him is received back tenfold.

"Kirby always has that little smile—and I truly believe dogs smile. He's 105 pounds now, all grown up. I'm so thankful he's so protective of my wife and daughters. That helps me sleep better at night when I'm not there. Bless him!"

Lee Ann Womack

"No matter what kind of day you've had, you come home and Ned is there, so happy to see you. And Sweetie, my cat, has been with me for years. When my younger child was born, Sweetie thought that Anna was her baby. She slept in the crib with her every single nap, and has slept at Anna's head since the first night we brought her home from the hospital. She'll let Anna do anything in the world to her. Anna puts her in the laundry hamper, the closet. . . . Just this morning I got up to take my oldest daughter, Aubre, to school, and Anna wanted to go with us because she knew we were going to get donuts. I heard her clomping around upstairs and then I heard her door shut. I thought, 'Well, good, then the animals won't go into her room.' When she came downstairs and announced to us that Sweetie was not in her closet, we all had a good laugh, 'cause then we knew exactly where Sweetie *was:* that rascal Anna had put Sweetie in her closet again. The moral to that story is that Sweetie always comes back for more; she thinks Anna can do no wrong.

"There's the two kids and Frank and me, but these animals complete our family. They really make our house a home. We have to keep lots of lint rollers around, though. We stand at the front door and line up and roll off before we go anywhere. On the tour bus, too, tons of lint rollers. We let our pets sleep with us—all four of us will be in our bed, and the dog and cats all piled up, too. So before we walk out the front door, we line up and do the roll!

"The kids learn so much about taking care of them and about how to respect other living beings. They are little teachers."

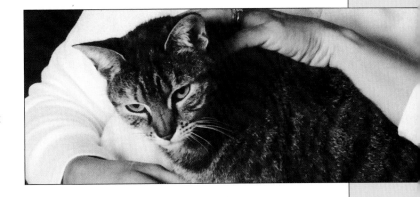

Darryl Worley

"I got Chazz for my wife, to protect her. He doesn't tolerate any intruders and won't let anyone in the house. As soon as they're inside, he'll kiss them and lick them and sit in their laps, but if they are on the outside of the house, no way—they are fair game. I named him after my favorite liquor store in Alabama when I was going to college.

"My wife, Beverly, had wanted a dog for a while, so my uncle got him for us from a guy in Jackson, Tennessee. He is so smart, very intelligent. He does this weird kind of talking with my wife; they have conversations. Sometimes in the middle of the night he'll hear something, and boy, does he let us know! I've pulled muscles, sitting straight up from being fast asleep.

"I've always felt that if people cannot commit to an animal, they shouldn't even think about getting one. We worry about Chazz if we're gonna be gone even for a day, because we came in one time and he was just a mess, trying to watch over the place for us. He'd lay down his life for us, I really think he would. The way you treat them tells them how you feel about them."

Chely Wright

"She's my constant companion, my traveling companion, you name it, she's there. She goes everywhere with me. I carry her around in a big purse, and when no one is looking I take her out. Miss Minnie is a tiny Yorkshire named after my dear friend and mentor Minnie Pearl. She is an awesome bus buddy. She's been properly trained, so when the bus is rolling and nature calls, she's got it all under control.

"She's my little soul mate. Wet nose, fur, and a wagging tail and all. The only time I leave her behind is when I travel internationally, and I hate that. Oh, I love her so much."

Tammy Wynette

"Tammy loved that little dog. I don't remember ever seeing her without him—even when we were working, she always had him. Richey usually carried him; I think he was just part of the package. He thought he was a big ol' German shepherd, always on the attack and growling at any new face. I know he was a comfort to her when she felt like she was the only one in the world, some of those dark, painful nights. He was the only one in the world who loved her without conditions, never even aware of her one-of-a-kind voice, or the gift she gave us all when she sang.

"Tammy, Killer misses you, and me and the whole world does, too!"

In memory of my dear friend.
—Tanya Tucker

Wynonna

"I have fourteen dogs, and I believe they chose me. I've rescued a lot of them. I've been known to stop traffic and jump out of the car to save one. I've acquired them at gas stations, grocery stores, and parking lots. Sometimes they just show up. I think the animals nearby get together and talk about what great snacks I have; they know that I'm snack heaven!

"I had a dog named Loretta Lynn that was with me for twenty years. We traveled the world together. She always sat beside me in the studio when I made a record, and when I went to television shows she would sit in the dressing room waiting for me. If I went to visit family, they knew to expect her. She even sat in a limo while I went to the White House to visit President Bush, Sr. and Barbara. I think church was the only place that she didn't go.

"Shortly after Loretta turned twenty years old, she became ill. Even though she was not feeling well, she always wagged her tail to go with me on tour. She would lie in her bed next to me while I put on my makeup before a show, and afterwards, late at night, she would sit beside me as we cruised on the bus.

"Memorial Day weekend, we were home again, and one morning I opened the door to let her out. I sat at my desk looking through my mail, and after ten or fifteen minutes I noticed that she hadn't come back inside, so I went to look for her. I live on top of a mountain and Loretta was so old that she couldn't walk or see very well, and she certainly could not have gone very far. I searched for her for hours, and the feeling overwhelmed me that she was no longer here. I never saw Loretta again. It was as if she didn't want to burden me with the sorrow of having to bury her. She must have worked out a deal with a hawk or an owl; I think she was carried away.

"I went and sat on my swing on the porch, and as I looked out over the land I realized that she was gone forever. Whenever I walk out on the farm, I feel her presence and I know she's waiting for me on the other side.

"On November 22, 2003, I got married. During my vows to my husband I promised, 'I will be as affectionate with you as I am with our pets.' The congregation chuckled, but they know how passionate I am about my animals. My favorite thing to do in winter is to gather all of my pets and place them all around me on my oversized comfy chair next to the fireplace. I can get four in the chair and my two big dogs at my feet and my two cats on either side of my head, purring in my ears. I'm in complete ecstasy! When it's warm outside, my favorite thing to do is to sit out on the back porch and have them all lay around me while they sun themselves. I sit with treats and as I call out their names they lift their heads to catch the treats. Now, that's life!

"When I travel on airplanes, I always take one dog with me onboard. When I travel on the bus, I take up to three dogs. I always love to see the look on people's faces as they come up on the bus for meet-and-greets. Sometimes the children are very shy and I enjoy watching them come out of their shell because the dogs are so welcoming. Angel, my rat terrier, is a social butterfly and enjoys kissing everyone who comes onboard. And I love putting the dogs on the bed with me in the hotel room to watch a movie, then order room service. The room service guy always gets a kick out of me chopping up the chicken and rice to give to the dogs.

"My favorite thing to do when I'm home is to load my dogs in my Suburban (I can get up to seven inside) and cruise through my small town. I roll all the windows down and enjoy watching people wave and laugh. Sometimes I can hear them say, 'There goes Wy-noah.' I cruise up to the farm and take the dogs to the lake. I get such joy out of watching them get so dirty; it's so freeing. When I get home, I put them in the shower with me and I'm proud to say I can wash up to seven dogs in one hour!

"I love the saying 'all creatures great and small.' I believe God created everything and that all life matters, however great and small. I try to be a teacher, not a preacher, but it has always been my belief that it is my job to take care of those who are helpless, to be a voice for those who cannot speak. I carry rubber gloves in my car and when I see a dead animal I will pull over and help remove that animal from the road. I believe they deserve this.

"I tell people to remember that although our pets cannot tell us what they need with their voices, they can show us with their actions. It's up to us to pay close attention to the signs they give us. If they're lagging behind

166

on a walk or they are reluctant to jump on the bed, or if you notice they are slow to get up after a nap or if they lick their joints, they're trying to tell you that they're in pain. Follow your heart and listen to your gut instinct. And take them to your vet for general checkups; we are their caretakers as well as their masters.

"I'm thankful that when I come home, they're sitting at my door waiting to greet me, no matter what shape I'm in. I love what I do and I love to give, but sometimes I come home spiritually, emotionally, and physically bankrupt. Whether my records are platinum or plywood, and whether I'm #1 or #101 on the charts, they couldn't care less because they love me for who I am, not what I do. When I'm down or when I'm having a rough day, sometimes I'll go and sit by myself. One by one, they will come and gather around me. It's as if they tune into what I need, and their companionship heals me. And when I look into their eyes, I know I am loved. My animals have taught me patience and compassion. They've taught me to never give up on someone I love, and that love never fails. To give is to receive."

Trisha Yearwood

"**R**oseanne is a mutt. She is the product of a long love affair between a chow and a German shepherd who kept getting out of his yard. They had two litters of puppies together, and her litter was pound-bound when I got her.

"She is like a child to me. Her love is completely unconditional, and she's been through so much with me. I always joke that she's my longest lasting relationship! I got her when she was just eight weeks old, long before I started making music for a living. She's been through everything with me. She has taught me so much about love, and has been the greatest companion a girl could ever ask for. To know that there is someone in your life that will protect you, die for you, and love you, and who knows that you will do the same for her, is a magical thing. Roseanne and I share a truly special bond.

"Like children, animals cannot take care of themselves. They rely on us to do that for them and we have to take that as a serious responsibility. If you have the space and the time to devote to owning a pet, I would urge you to go to a shelter and get one . . . or seven! Everyone says that mutts make the best pets, and I have to agree!

"Roseanne is such a great friend to me, and I love her with all my heart and soul."

This page is lovingly dedicated to the memory of Roseanne, who passed away on November 19, 2003 at the age of 15.

Acknowledgments

Karen Will Rogers

Mom, thank you for your love, support, and belief in my dream to be a photographer, and for my first camera. Words could never describe all you gave to me in my life. Thanks for the great gifts of pets in our family. I love you.

Dad, I know you're proud of all of my accomplishments, as I am of yours. You gave to your family, friends and country. You'll see the book in your heart from heaven. That brings comfort and warmth to my soul. I miss you and I love you. Oh and by the way, the cats thank you for the heating pads for the winter!

Robert, Lori, Brittany, Ashley, Christopher, and Johnny Williams, your part in this fueled my fire to finish this book. I love you.

My brother John, for the amazing website, your love and enthusiasm. Glad you are part of this dream come true. I love you, too!

To Rose Hein and Tracy Williams, we have a common bond: pets, humor, love, creativity, and a lot of history. "The best thing I got out of high school was you." You bless my life; I love you both.

Carol and Billy Roach, your love, energy, and friendship are such a great gift. I love you. John Zoppa, shadows never leave a person, people do. Life's journeys bring people back like you. Your support, I felt in my heart, and our love for animals brought us closer. I love you.

Brandon Giles, thank you so much for your love, support, and under-standing. You made me smile when I was tired; you forgave me when I was cranky. You called me with your magic talking cat and made me laugh. You're in my heart and you fill my soul and I love you.

Laura Lacy, I prayed for someone like you. I am so grateful our paths crossed. Your passion for life, animals, and people is exceptional. This is really real. You made this process a "Lucy and Ethel" episode; we laughed until we could laugh no more. I love you. Sherri T. Gray, I'll never forget your grace, support, and friendship. Thanks for being there when I needed someone to talk to. I love you.

Ashley Giles, you sat on the floor with me as we sorted photographs on those late nights! I thank you for your help and soulful dedication to animals. Your light shines so bright. I love you.

Jim Cauley, the tooth angel! You're very special. Your support and grace will never be forgotten. I love you.

Larry Hill, thank you so much for all your help. You give your all so unconditionally, and I am grateful for the many times you rose to the occasion.

Jim Ortale, thank you for being my friend and my brother. I love you.

Karen Russell, for Lobo's dog collar; it's the best!

A big thanks to Baxter Buck for your help with those book photo shoots. Your friendship is greatly valued.

To the great Norman Vincent Peale, for influencing my life in the most positive and productive ways. I am grateful for all of your tools. I've learned from you many of life's greatest lessons. Thank you.

To my dogs, Wilson and Maggie, you are pure love, loyal, and endless entertainment. You amaze me with how you love. I wish I were wired like that. I see what you do for my world, and I am moved. Your love fed my soul through this whole process. You don't speak, but I hear you in my heart. It's a sound I can't live without.

To Robert, my cat, you couch potato, food hog eatin', present bringin' mess of a fat cat. I love you, furry man, but could you get a job to support your over-eating habit!

With gratitude, we would like to thank David Nuding for taking the book to Simon and Schuster. Thank you for your sharp business sense and your friendship.

Laura Lacy

To my brilliant parents, who have taught me love, sharing, giving, and the capacity to care for others, including our many pets over the years. I love you both very much. Dad, you kept us going on many a tough day with your words of infinite wisdom: "Hey, if you pull at something long enough it's bound to come loose." To my amazing sister, Claudia Lacy Kelly, thank you for all the valuable advice, support, and for being the best sister ever. I love you. To my nephew, Conor, you have been blessed by the shutterbug: enjoy your talent and live through the lens; it is a fascinating and magical place. My niece, Lacy, thank you for always making me feel so special. I love you both very much.

To my "oldest and dearest" friend, Donna Dixon Aykroyd, I love you so much, oh wise one. Your love, nurturing, and brilliance have forever made my life a better place to be. Dan Aykroyd, I am forever grateful for your love of life, history, and all things great and meaningful, and your overwhelming generosity to include me along the way. To my goddaughter, Stella, I love you so much; thanks for picking me!

Joshua Ragsdale, you see the soul and love so completely. I am so blessed to have you in my life. Your love of animals knows no boundaries. I love you, my friend.

My brother-friend, Charlie Daniels Jr., thank you for embracing me and being a dear, sweet friend and a true animal lover. I love you.

To one of the brightest stars ever, Katie Cook. What a true blessing you have been in my life. I love you, too! Thank you for your deep commitment to animals. Shine on.

To a man who made a huge impact on my life, Mr. Sam Haskell: thank you for sharing your life story and great wisdom; you are awesome.

Dr. James Cauley, what a gift you are. A special wonderful friend. Thank you for being so completely supportive of me in love and life. I love you dearly. I'll give you the other half back later!

My dear friend Leah Taylor, thank you for all your support and valued advice. I love you.

To Tony Quinn, timing is everything in life. Thank you for being there. You will never know how much your presence has meant. Love and thanks.

To my home girls in Virginia, Lucy Scott, Janie Collins, and Karin Viera, I love my "Seestors." To all the memories and all the pet parties; I love you gals! De Bears! To Tanya Tucker, thank you for all the experience and knowledge I gained working for you; you are a wonderful person with a heart of gold. Thank you for your willingness to help and contribute. I love you!

Roni Larsen, my country music mentor. I am so glad you made me buy tickets to Wynonna, Trisha, Reba, and John Michael. I love you. In loving memory of Chloe. To the Dixon family, Earl, Mary Ruth, Hillbilly

Heaven, Roy and Diane, for many years of great country music—I love you all!

To my partner in this book, Karen Will Rogers, we did it! Thank you for asking me to join you in this endeavor. It has been a true honor and a real privilege. You are not only a dear friend, but also one of the most passionate people I know. Your dedication to this book has been unstoppable, and your love of animals, pure and immeasurable. I admire so much what you have accomplished. I love you, my friend.

Flo Boyd, thank you a million times for providing me with one of the best things that ever happened to me, my Lucy Belle.

To Bryan Frasher, you define the word friend. Thank you for being so kind in many a difficult and trying situation, especially saying good-bye to Lucy. Patience is golden and that, you are. I love you.

Bascha Satin, thank you for all the support, French, and Yiddish lessons! I am grateful for your friendship and your love of life; thanks for all the good laughs! *Compei!*

And last, but certainly not least, in loving memory of my devoted and loving companion of thirteen years, Lucy Belle Lacy, the most wonderfully perfect ChowChow God ever created. You were and always will be part of my reason for doing this book. You were a constant source of inspiration and I miss you deeply and dearly every day. I know that you are blissfully happy sniffing pine needles and chasing squirrels in heaven; this one's for you, ol' girl!

To our publishing company, Simon and Schuster, and our editor, Micki Nuding of the Pocket Books division; you are a dream come true. Thank you for all of your advice, knowledge, and brilliant input along the way.

CMT, one of the most powerful voices in country music today, we thank you for aligning with us and sharing our vision. We look forward to being part of the MTV Networks family and creating big things for our country music fans!

Thanks to our attorney, Philip Lyon of Jack, Lyon and Jones. You embraced this project with passion and a personal commitment, and we are grateful to you for your continued hard work.

To Hilary and Allen Butler, who stood behind this project and gave it credibility, a home, and a foundation. And Hilary, for her commitment and continued hard work with the ACT NOW program. We thank you both.

We would humbly and gratefully like to thank Lorrie Morgan for her passion, energy, and time in assisting us with the fight for a new shelter in Nashville, which we are proud to say is up and running very successfully. Thank you, Lorrie!

We would like to thank the following people for being generous of their time and energy: George Armistead, Kathi Atwood, Lynn Bennett, Stephen L. Betts, editor in chief of *CMToday* magazine, Ann Beutler, Jill and Billy Block, Jason Blume, Lisa Boullt, Jeff Bowen, Governor Phil Bredesen, Mark Bright, Tony and Anastasia Brown, Larry Bryant, Mickey Bryant, Laura Bryna, Nancy Burton, Mary Lou Cathy, Robert Cheatam, Chip Stone, and all the folks on the City Council of Nashville, especially Sharon Corbitt, Courtney Crist, Kimber Cuffe, Tish Cyrus, Lora Daniels, Paige and Dillion Dixon, Al and Tracy Embry, Fletcher Foster, Fran and Joe Galante, Billy Galvin, Wanda Garrison, Kate Garvey, Bill Gatzimos, Harris Gilbert, guerrilla design, Cain Hall, Pam Harbert, Anita Hogin, Chuck Howard, Paul Jeffers, Michael Johnathan, Bruce Johnson, Mitch Johnson, Nancy Jones, Karen Karan, Jennifer Kemp, Nicole Kopperud of *Country Weekly*, Judy Ladebauche, Luellyn Latocki of Latocki Team Creative, Ken Leiser, Natalie Maines, and Janis Sontany. Also, Louise Mandrell and her entire staff, especially Sande Weiss, Gary Manlove and Champion, Kris Marcy, Paul McKelvey and Cayte Nobles of Durys camera store, Donna McKenzie, Jeff McMahon, Susan Myers, Melissa Miggo, Regina Moore, Stan Moress, Joshua Motohashi, Devon O'Day, Patrick D. O'Rourke, Lamar Raley, Debbie Randle, Jonni Hartman Rogers, Karen Russell, Tim Schumacher, John Seals for allowing us to witness a horrific situation that so desperately needed to be revealed, Lisa Seals, Garth Shaw, Eric Silver, Rob Simbeck, Verb Simpson, Jennifer Stoughton, Regina Stuve, The Do, The Scene, Preshias Tomes, Kathy Walker, Kurt Webster, Shawn Williams, Debra Wingo, Paul Worley, The Hermitage Hotel, Nashville, and Greg Sligh for your support and flexibility, thank you! CMT Most Wanted Live and the crew!

A very special and loving thank you to our friend and gifted photographer, Nancy Lee Andrews, for all of her help and advice. Your contributions were endless. We love you. Thank you to our dear friend Emmy Harris, who made herself available to do make-up when necessary. Your work is flawless. We love you, Em!

Sandi Kight, our wonderful assistant, thank you for all your hard work and flexibility. With the voice of an angel, keep singing. We love you.

Our brother Robert Weedman. Oh man, where do we begin!! Thank you for your incredible knowledge of the country music business, your willingness to always always do research, ask questions, and give advice. You are invaluable. Thank you, we love you.

Cheri Hancock, you are a true animal saint and we are grateful to have had you helping us. We love you and thank you!

To our friend Holly Hefner, you are truly a devoted and dedicated advocate of the animal world. Thank you for your love and support.

To one of the greatest characters of our time and a leading authority on animals, "Jungle Jack" Hanna. Thank you for your lifetime of entertainment and commitment to animals near and far. Your dedication and knowledge are astonishing. You are truly one with nature.

About the Authors

KAREN WILL ROGERS moved to Nashville eight years ago from Los Angeles. A professional photographer for fifteen years, Karen's work includes head shots, production stills, publicity, CD covers, fine arts, modeling, musicians, concerts, and commercial and wedding photography. Her love for music and animals inspired this project, capturing the essence of the celebrities' relationships with their pets, and expressing the love and spiritual bonds people have with them. If these pictures encourage just one person to adopt a pet or to get their animals spayed and neutered, then she's accomplished her goal.

LAURA LACY, a native Virginian, comes to this project by way of New York and Los Angeles. After running her own event-planning company for executives and celebrities, Lacy held diverse positions in the entertainment industry, including assistant to the stars, art direction, styling, and production. When she moved to Nashville to work in country music, her deep love of animals and people led her to this project. She is grateful that so many of country music's brightest stars share her dedication to improving the lives of animals.